HEADINGLEY

Headingley

JOHN MARSHALL

PELHAM BOOKS

First published in Great Britain by
PELHAM BOOKS LTD
52 Bedford Square
London, W.C.1
1970

7207 0359 X

Printed in Great Britain by
Western Printing Services Ltd, Bristol

ACKNOWLEDGEMENTS

I wish to thank, most sincerely, all those officials and members of the Yorkshire County Cricket Club and others who have given me most generous help in the compilation of this book and, in particular, Mr J. H. Nash, Mr D. B. Close, Mr W. E. Bowes, Mr J. M. Kilburn, Mr Ron Yeomans, Mr Wilfred Rhodes, Mr Arthur Wood, Mr Norman Shuttleworth, Mr Colin Cowdrey, Mr John Arlott and Mr Frank Lee. I also wish to acknowledge the following valuable sources: *Wisden Cricketers' Almanack*; *Yorkshire C.C.C. Year Books*; *The Watney Book of Test Match Grounds* by I. A. R. Peebles; *History of Yorkshire Cricket, 1833–1903* by Rev. R. S. Holmes; *History of Yorkshire County Cricket, 1903–1923* by A. W. Pullin ('Old Ebor'); *History of Yorkshire County Cricket, 1924–1949* by J. M. Kilburn; *The Summer Game* and *Good Days* by Neville Cardus; *Forty Years of English Cricket* by H. W. Lee and Laurence Thompson; *Hirst and Rhodes*, *Cricket Bouquet* and *Cricketers of My Times* by A. A. Thomson; *Best Cricket Stories* (edited), *Game of a Lifetime*, *Test Matches of 1964* and *The Match I Remember* by Denzil Batchelor; *Jackson's Year* by Alan Gibson; *Cricket* and *Fast Fury* by Freddie Trueman; *A History of Cricket* by H. S. Altham and E. W. Swanton; *Express Deliveries* by Bill Bowes; *Wilfred Rhodes* by Sidney Rogerson; *Gone to the Test Match*, *Test Match Diary 1953* and *Vintage Summer 1947* by John Arlott; *Great Cricket Matches* edited by Handasyde Buchanan; *Aussies and Ashes* by Bill Bowes; *The Phoenix History of Cricket* by Roy Webber; *The Headingley Story* (volume 1—rugby) edited by Ken Dalby; *The Challenging Tests* by Ray Lindwall; *Just My Story* by Len Hutton; *The History of Cricket* by Eric Parker; *Cricket Triumphs and Troubles* by Cecil Parkin.

CONTENTS

ILLUSTRATIONS

ACKNOWLEDGEMENTS

The Author's thanks are due to the following, whose photographs are reproduced in this book:
Central Press Photos: 6, 7, 8, 9, 11, 12, 13, 14, 15, 16, 20, 22. *P.A.–Reuter:* 10, 17. *Sport & General:* 18, 19, 23. *Daily Mail:* 21.

1 'Lot 17a'

Like other famous institutions, notably the liner *Queen Mary*, which started life as '534', Headingley, one of the world's best known sports grounds, was once just a number. It was, prosaically, 'Lot 17a', a parcel of land forming part of Cardigan Fields at the sale, in 1888, of the Cardigan estates, a few minutes' buggy ride from the centre of Leeds.

The St John's Club had, since its foundation in 1870, played football upon Cardigan Fields—achieving fame in the North as the 'Amber and Blues'—but there was no sports ground in the City to compete for the big events, in particular those comparatively new national attractions, cricket Test matches, with such noted arenas as Lord's in the South, Trent Bridge in the Midlands, and Old Trafford 'over the border'. So it was that leading businessmen, imbued with fine sporting instincts, clear vision and deep civic pride, banded together, agreed to buy 'Lot 17a', and resolved to transform it into the most splendid cricket and football enclosure in all Britain. These far-seeing sportsmen, happily possessed of much 'brass' as well as business acumen and bold spirits, formed the Leeds Cricket, Football and Athletic Co., Ltd., which owns the ground to this day.

Their names deserve to be recorded—Lord Hawke, one of the Yorkshire County Cricket Club's greatest, and certainly longest serving of captains, was Chairman, and Mr C. F. Tetley, bearer of a name which means good beer to all true Yorkshiremen, was Vice-Chairman. Their fellow directors were Mr J. W. Bannister, Mr F. H. Barr, Mr George Bray, Mr W. L. Jackson M.P. (father of F.S., later Sir Stanley Jackson, one of the greatest of all-round cricketers), Mr F. Lawson, Mr John Gordon jun., Mr J. Tweedale, Mr W. B. Nicholson and Mr J. Watmough. The imaginative gesture of these gentlemen fired others as the years went by, one outstanding for his zeal in the modern development of Headingley being Sir Edwin Airey, of the construction firm, William Airey and Sons. He became Chairman of the company in 1923 and devoted 32 years to the establishment of the Headingley ground, or rather grounds, as world-renowned international sports venues. They are, in fact, recognised as his memorial and the visitor enquiring into the history of the place is likely, early in the discussions to have quoted to him (as I did, by Mr John Nash, the energetic and dedicated secretary of Yorkshire C.C.C.) the epitaph for Sir Christopher Wren in St Paul's Cathedral: 'If you would see his memorial, look around you'.

Southern folk might fairly claim that Lord's is the most illustrious of all cricket grounds with the longest, proudest traditions, as well as the most fabulous pavilion; 'Brummagens' could argue that 'junior' Edgbaston is now the best equipped. But none can dispute that Headingley, as a cricket *and* football ground, is unique. The main stand, known as 'the new stand', indeed serves both—a bulky, towering structure facing both ways, on one side surveying the cricket pitch, on the other, the football field. This giant replaced the former dual purpose stand, destroyed by fire on Good Friday in 1932. The builders were William Airey and Sons and the cost £20,000, a big sum for those days but nevertheless accepted by the club as a noble gesture, being far less than an 'outside' firm with no affectionate links would have charged.

Leeds St John's as such expired in the season 1889–90, becoming instead the football section of the Leeds Cricket, Football and Athletic Co. Ltd. The first match at Headingley, scene of so many Yorkshire and England triumphs and tribulations both at cricket and Rugby League football, took place on September 20 1890. The new Leeds football team, in terra cotta and green jerseys, played Mannington and won by a dropped goal and a try to nil.

In fact the first code used on the Headingley ground was Rugby Union, with the same number of players, fifteen per side, and the same method of scoring, as in the south. In the season 1897–8 the method of scoring was changed to that of the Rugby League, and in the 1906–7 season the transition was completed with a reduction to thirteen players a side. On that 'other side' of the grandstand some notable individual feats have been recorded. In 1891–2, under Rugby Union rules, J. H. Potter, sole remaining link with the Leeds St John's finalists of 1887, kicked twelve goals in a match, a club record which was equalled but never beaten. E. Harris, who first played for Leeds against Featherstone Rovers in 1930, scored more than thirty tries in each of seven seasons, his highest being 63 and 58. His aggregate was a career record of 391 tries with a total of 1,169 points to his credit.

During the season 1950-1, H. E. Cook had the astounding record of 150 goals, including twelve against York, the first team he played against for Leeds. J. F. Thompson, in 390 appearances from 1923 onwards, kicked 862 goals and collected a total of 1,883 points for his side. In the first sixty years at Headingley as a Rugby League club, Leeds played 1,026 matches, won 768, drew 48, lost 210 and scored 17,147 points against 6,955. A ground record was set up in 1952 when receipts from the England-Australia 'Test' were £8,628 12s. 6d. When Leeds played Bradford Northern in a League match in 1947 the attendance exceeded 40,000, also a record.

The Yorkshire County Cricket Club first played on their part of the ground in 1890. Before that the Bramall Lane ground at Sheffield —shared rather than divided for cricket and football, though the footballers charitably refrained from playing on the table—was the leading Yorkshire ground. It was not until 1903 that the Yorkshire C.C.C.'s headquarters were removed lock, stock and barrel, to Leeds. In its early days, though so near to the centre of Leeds, the Headingley ground wore a rural aspect and the lanes leading thence would echo, certainly upon Saturday afternoons, winter and summer, to the clip-clop of hooves, and of sturdy clogs too, as the wool masters drove there from their trim and prim red-brick Victorian homes and the men walked from their stark and narrow back-to-back dwellings in the little streets, saved from abject meanness only by the indomitable spirit of their inhabitants. Now one of those once pastoral approach routes, Kirkstall Lane, is known the world over or, at any rate, in all those parts of the world where an ear is lent to the radio when a Test match is being played at Headingley.

For bowlers, as you will hear from the commentators, bowl either from the Grandstand end or the Kirkstall Lane end, the latter being relished by many a fast bowler on account of the slope—not, perhaps, as pronounced as the Lord's slope but nevertheless so descending from north to south as to provide a clear distinction between bowling up it or down it. Though this declivity is not obvious to the eye of the spectator or even the fielder, the former will often be surprised and the latter dismayed, at the acceleration of the ball on its eager way to the Grandstand end. It has been known for a fielder thus frustrated to pick up the ball just over the white line and throw it in to the wicket as if a boundary had been narrowly saved. But the Headingley crowd, fair as to the Laws if demonstrably partisan as to

the result, will have none of that. The umpire may well have a
hundred signals and much verbal confirmation to aid him.

The wicket itself, apart from a spell which included the 1961 Test
against Australia, when it was fiercely criticised, has a reputation for
easy pace and goodwill to all batsmen, so that many, and without any
question whatever Sir Donald Bradman, remember it with warm
affection.

Yet the absence of conventional sight screens, especially in the
early stages of an innings, can make the sighting of the ball a matter
of some difficulty. At the northern, or Kirkstall Lane end there is
now an open stand which looks like a giant pew, the worshippers
within it showing only their heads as if they are upon their knees,
which may well be so in moments critical for Yorkshire teams or
Yorkshire players. Behind their heads and in front, concealing the
rest of them, is pale green boarding which serves as some screening
without unduly reducing the ground's capacity, and 'brass'-gathering
potential.

As for the Grandstand end, one member assured me that if the
powers installed the biggest sight screen ever constructed the batsman
at the other, higher, end would see over it and the gate receipts
would be disastrously down. Boarding helps but spectator discipline
is considered more effective. As the average Headingley spectator
feels as much part of the game as Boycott or Binks he tends to freeze
like a pointer as t'bowler runs up t'hill—and to freeze with a glare of
much ferocity anyone who dares to fidget. In recent years Headingley
has undergone some constructional changes, the most significant of
which, from the point of view of player-public relationship being the
resiting, upon the west side of the ground, at a cost of £24,000, of the
members' pavilion.

Now the players go to the wicket, and return from it, in splendid
isolation, their path leading, not through a throng of spectators as
heretofore, but from gate to pitch and back. Some there are who miss
the old back-slapping, hand-grabbing camaraderie of the more public
progress but others, I believe the majority, prefer the less direct
contact especially when attempting to concentrate upon the coming
duel as they walk to the crease. Incidentally, the old pavilion now
provides offices for the Secretariat, previously housed in Old Bank
Chambers, in the commercial heart of the thrusting City of Leeds.

More significant, from the point of view of future cricket prospects,
is the new winter shed at the Kirkstall Lane end, erected with the

help of a £10,000 legacy from a lady of true devotion, replacing a tea house wherein, with typical Yorkshire prudence, teaspoons were securely tethered. Here the embryo talent from all the Ridings sets out upon its hopeful, frequently anguished way to fame—or oblivion. 'That lad moves his feet like a good 'un'; 'Yon's a bowler if he stops ape-ing Freddie'; 'Ay, useful like—in't village team . . .'

All boys with cricket in their hearts are given a chance; all with cricket in their heads, hands and feet are given every encouragement. Even those from outside the county—though without hope of playing for it, so rigid is the qualification rule—may practise there.

And though no overseas player has yet appeared for Yorkshire, there is a distinct possibility that, say, a West Indian may yet do so. As in other English cities, coloured families from the Caribbean and other parts of the Commonwealth have settled in Leeds and there are now numbers of teenage sons, some with cricket in their blood, heart and sinews, who were born within a cricket-ball throw of the ground.

An innovation at Headingley which has no exact parallel in the sporting world is the plushy Leeds Taverners Club. Its elegant premises are spread over the first floor of the Grandstand, providing views, through huge picture windows, on one side of the cricket and on the other, the football. The Leeds Taverners Club has no point of comparison with the Lord's Taverners, the primary object of which convivial institution being to provide funds for the Playing Fields Association. The Leeds, or Headingley Taverners is purely a social club—officially described as 'a propretiary club of Leeds Cricket, Football and Athletic Company Limited'—and an exclusive one. Members are mostly prominent, and prosperous, local citizens, including the hierarchy of the Leeds C.F. and A. Co., which benefits from entrance fees and subscriptions, 50 guineas each.

As a guest of Mr Norman Shuttleworth, Chairman of the Club and a member of the Yorkshire C.C.C. Committee, I enjoyed as good a view as the ground provides of the Second Test match between England and the West Indies in July 1969. Looking down from this opulent eyrie with its deep pile carpets, bowls of massed flowers and well-stocked bar, the red brick vista at the Kirkstall Lane end is nicely mellowed by two platoons (each eighteen strong) of poplars, the ample foliage of which dances prettily in the breeze. An attempt to recapture the rural aspect of bygone days? Not exactly. The trees, a quick-growing variety, were planted by the practical

Yorkshire administrators with 'brass' for the Club very much in mind. It had been the habit of the Yorkshire folk living round the ground not only to watch the proceedings therein for nothing, but to invite their friends and relations to share their balconies for this free show. The result was that the clicking of the Headingley turnstiles was often less than merry. Now the ringside inhabitants must pay like folks from further afield, or see nothing. There were rather more poplars before the new winter shed went up; this now shares the protective duty.

One name, famous outside Yorkshire as well as in its centre, stands out boldly inside the ground at its northerly end—Hepworths. This must be a source of some gratification to Mr Shuttleworth as he sits in his accustomed place in the Taverners Club, for he is that widely known multiple tailoring firm's Managing Director. It is, however, a source of some embarrassment to the B.B.C. whose cameramen must seek to exclude it from their lenses as advertising is not encouraged at Broadcasting House. Should this delicate subject be raised the rejoinder is likely to be: 'Well, what about Pickles?' This name may also be seen—just outside the ground. A Yorkshire name, to be sure, belonging at this advantageous spot, to an enterprising shopkeeper.

Green, in spite of the dry summer, was the cricket ground, but greener still the Rugby ground which I contemplated from the Taverners Club. The latter, indeed, looked as lush and well-groomed as the lawn of a stately mansion, the reason being the elaborate and expensive irrigation, drainage and heating precautions taken to ensure that play is always possible upon its surface. Even when snow lies thick upon the roads and rooftops all around, the strip is as green and resilient as ever.

For, beneath its surface there are 38 miles of wires to carry the electric current which mocks the most Arctic conditions. Why, oh! why, cannot an adaptation of this admirable system be devised to dry out from below the cricket ground when the rain that inevitably at some time stops play, has itself stopped? Beautiful is this cosseted turf, as I found when I trod it on my way, by means of a mountainous climb up the Rugby side of the Grandstand, to the broadcasting commentary box, tucked snugly under the very eaves, like the nest of a house-martin. And not a lot roomier. With John Arlott, Brian Johnston, Trevor Bailey, old uncle Jim Swanton and all in occupation the house-martin's residence would seem spacious in comparison.

The viewpoint, however, is generally held to be admirable. You look straight down the length of the pitch from behind the bowler running up the south to north slope. The cameramen occupy the highest spot of all, a platform on the roof above the commentary box. The Press have their premises above the Taverners Club, commodious compared with the commentary box, with refreshment facilities including a bar to the rear of the glassed-in Press box itself. An interesting aspect of this rendezvous is the presence of so many famous cricketers who have substituted the ball-pen for the ball.

Indeed on some occasions a most distinguished team of varied epochs could be mustered, including (at the time of my visit) Bill Bowes, since his playing days a professional journalist of much skill, Ian Peebles, whose writing on cricket is both evocative and humorous, Keith Miller and E. M. Wellings, old Fleet Street as well as cricketing campaigners, Jim Laker, Ken Barrington, and Colin Milburn. Deep down below, at the very bottom of the stand, is the Players' club room, its motif the Rugby club's colours, its sideboard completely covered with silver trophies of very considerable market value, silver prices being what they are, apart from the honour and glory they have brought to Headingley.

But it is outside, around the ground and among the spectators, that the real atmosphere of Headingley is liable to invade you, the winter crowds upon the Rugby side rather more clamorous but sharing the fervour and Yorkshire-above-all spirit of those assembling in summer upon 'the other side' whether for a Test match, a county match or the swift-paced, over-limited League cricket matches enlivening Saturday afternoons. A bit higgledy-piggledy to be frank, inclining towards the positively tatty when it comes to the cavernous bars where the draught beers and the bottled beers are segregated and no glimpse of the cricket may be had. You may take your pint of Tetley's or Magnet ale out on to the concrete behind the places 'reserved for wounded warriors' but there is no encouragement to do so as there is at Lord's with its Taverners' bar open to the ground.

You go to Headingley to watch the game, and watching it with one elbow on a bar is not provided for. To supplement on-the-spot comforts such as Tetley and tea, most of the Headingley regulars arrive prepared for all contingencies, with enough food for all day, caps and macs and newspapers (to sit on, not to read), cushions, folding stools and binoculars. The really well-prepared Headingley spectator, especially on the Saturday of a big match, when nothing will shift him from his place, looks like an itinerant junkman, or junkwoman. For the female of the species is as zealous as the male, if not more so. There was one, I recall, all Yorkshire from adequately covered top to sturdily shod toe, who must surely qualify for the 'most complete Headingley supporter' award were one offered.

She wore a beret and an ankle length raincoat belted securely. She had a shopping bag filled to the gaping brim with sustaining provender such as the home-baked bread and cakes for which Yorkshire housewives are justly renowned, and a rucksack which, I suspected, contained reserve rations. She had flasks and a brolly, papers in sufficient numbers to cover herself entirely if it should rain, and a folding chair which she placed resolutely close to a B.B.C. colour TV camera beside the pavilion.

She bestowed upon the cameraman a look which clearly bade him budge up and make room, the interloper. He obliged. Beside the lady's right foot there sat a dog, a Yorkshire terrier of pure descent, watching the play with the quizzical, knowing expression to be observed upon some thousands of human faces. Beside the lady's left foot was a transistor radio tuned, it is perhaps needless to record, to the commentary from the Grandstand's heights. She was not going to miss anything at all, any more than was the earnest youth nearby, recording in an outsize scorebook every ball bowled, every run made. Serious but not entirely dour, the Headingley crowd, unlike any other. Proud, intensely proud to be Yorkshire folk in Yorkshire and even more particularly, Leeds folk in Leeds.

For, after all, as quite a number of them took the trouble to point out in the intervals (you don't chatter when t'play's on) at the end of the winter 1968-9 this remarkable tally of honours had been achieved:—the Leeds Rugby Club had won the Rugby League cup at Wembley, the Rugby League Leader's trophy, the Yorkshire League championship and the Yorkshire cup. Yorkshire had won the County Cricket Championship and Yorkshire 2nd XI the Minor Counties championship (the first time this double had been accomplished). And Leeds United had won the Football League championship, a gradely grand slam, by Gow!

2 *The Dedicated Ones*

A cockney friend of mine, serving in His Majesty King George the VIth's Forces, found himself stationed in a Yorkshire town with the pleasant name of Slaithwaite, inexplicably corrupted to sound soggily like Slowit—a town whose cricket team was once dismissed for one run by Kirkheaton, the bowlers sharing this triumph bearing the names George Herbert Hirst and Wilfred Rhodes.

My friend was, at the time, an N.C.O. and captain of his unit's cricket team, for which his commanding officer from time to time turned out. One day, with a keen match in prospect, the C.O. told the skipper that he was dubious as to whether or not he would be well enough to play as malaria had taken its accustomed toll of his energies, 'Either you are fit and can play, or unfit and cannot play, sir,' said the corporal uncompromisingly. The colonel curtly replied that certainly he would play. He was promptly requested by the corporal to open the bowling, which he did with some success. The skipper had no doubt in his mind that he would be stripped or, at the least, posted for his defiance. Instead he received notification that he had been recommended for OCTU, the C.O. having perceived in him leadership potential. The C.O., as his compatriots will readily recognise, was a Yorkshireman, dyed in the wool, dedicated, cast in the mould of leaders like Lord Hawke and Mr Brian Sellers.

He would no more have had an unfit man in his side than would either of those gentlemen when they were captaining the Yorkshire side. Brian Sellers, son of Arthur Sellers, a sound batsman who played for the county between 1899 and 1918, took over the captaincy from F. E. Greenwood in 1933 and held it until the end of the 1947 season. He was the toughest disciplinarian since Lord Hawke and, under him, Yorkshire became more fiercely aggressive than ever, especially in their superb fielding. The influence of Brian Sellers upon Yorkshire has been profound, his devotion lifelong. He typifies, more than any other Yorkshire cricketer, perhaps, Yorkshire determination, pride and almost compulsive supremacy. As a boy he

captained the XI at St Peter's School, York. Even then he was
preparing himself—though it seemed at the time an unattainable
ambition—for the greatest task and the highest honour for a
Yorkshireman in the world of cricket, the captaincy of Yorkshire.
Ron Yeomans, a member of the Yorkshire C.C.C. Committee,
played under him in that school side in the 1920s. At Headingley he
recalled to me that young Sellers was very insistent upon discipline
and good fielding, a good fielder always receiving preference over one
less reliable even if marginally a better bat or bowler. This stern
insistence on the highest standards he manifests to this day.

As chairman of the Cricket Committee he will permit no slackness
or sloppiness. When Freddie Trueman, towards the end of his
illustrious career, grew whiskers for a film appearance he was told to
shave them off or stand down from the team. Happily Freddie was
'shot' before this drastic measure could be carried out. Good
appearance ('spick, span and spiked') he regards as an essential
aspect of true discipline, which means Yorkshire discipline. As
captain he would not allow his team to wear any but Yorkshire
blazers and sweaters when playing in county matches. 'You are
playing for Yorkshire, not England' he would tell his Test stars, as if
getting the priorities in perspective. He would also insist upon all
members of his team washing their hands before going in to tea. And
once, when an old cricketer of some eminence was stowing his
flannels in his cricket bag Sellers told him, quietly but firmly, to fold
them properly.

Yet, meeting Brian Sellers off duty, as I did during that 1969
Headingley Test against the West Indies (he is always on duty when
Yorkshire are playing) you would never suspect the inexorable
streak. He is a man of much charm, big, amiable, an easy talker with
a friendly smile. As a player, his contributions to his team's success,
especially in his exemplary fielding, were considerable, though he was
never considered to be quite Test class.

He played 386 innings for Yorkshire, aggregating nearly 9,000 runs
with an average of 23·18 (compared with his father's 18·43; oddly
enough, both in their county careers, took just eight wickets, those of
Sellers snr. being much the more economical). But his place among
the great Yorkshire captains is not in dispute. Six times he led the
side to the Championship and in every year of his captaincy Yorkshire were well up in the top half of the County Championship table.
Was he the greatest captain of them all? Some insist that he was,

though Lord Hawke has many supporters still and Brian Close is in the list.

One veteran member of the Yorkshire club ventured to me the opinion that if the merits of Sellers and Norman Yardley could have been combined there would have emerged the finest captain of all times—'Sellers the strict disciplinarian and Yardley the easy-going, who commanded respect by his performances and personal example rather than unrelenting firmness.' Yardley was, unquestionably, the better player. His 364 innings for Yorkshire between 1936 and 1955 yielded 11,632 runs with an average of 31·95 and he took 192 wickets costing 30·29 runs each. He also played in twenty Test matches, captured Bradman's wicket three times running during the 1946–7 tour, headed the bowling averages when captain of England in 1948 and hit a century for Cambridge in the University match.

Yorkshire born, of course, like all his predecessors, including the present President, Sir William Worsley, father of the Duchess of Kent, was captain from 1925 to 1927. All his predecessors? There was one exception—of all people Lord Hawke. But as he was born abroad while his father was on service and the family roots were deep in the county this was regarded as a technicality. Still today the mere whispered suggestion of a non-Yorkshire captain would be treated with the scorn that would have, in the days before Gentlemen and Players became just cricketers, greeted the suggestion of a professional captain of England. Absolutely not done in Yorkshire, whatever those other counties of low calibre and lower pride, chose to do. Nor is any player from outside the county permitted to play for it.

The unforgiveable sin has, in fact, been committed and though the awful gaffe was long ago it is still tactless to mention the name of Cecil Parkin. This great player any other county would have held on to with much tenacity, was born on February 18, 1886, at Egglescliffe, which is near Yarm-on-Tees and a matter of yards only outside the Yorkshire boundary. Young Parkin was first played for his batting and fielding, not for the bowling which brought him international fame. For Ossett, a Yorkshire Council club he scored 45 against Dewsbury and promptly signed on.

The next season, 1906, he was tried as a fast bowler and took 116 wickets, the highest number in the League. This feat caused him to be 'noticed' and he was picked to play for Yorkshire against Gloucestershire at Headingley. On the morning of the match he was interviewed by Lord Hawke and told him that he had been born just inside Durham. His Lordship, possibly remembering his own arrival in exile, had already heard the news and decided to defy tradition. 'We are not particular about a few yards—you play today,' he told Parkin. Not particular! In that debut match at Leeds Parkin made an inauspicious start with a duck and a couple of wickets (he was to take a few more as a visitor in the years to come) then descended to Yorkshire's second XI where nemesis quickly overtook him.

He received a telegram from Mr F.C. (later Sir Frederick) Toone, the Yorkshire secretary for 28 years, which said: 'Objection to qualification; letter follows.' Parkin decided, without waiting for the letter, to seek an appointment elsewhere. He was formally notified that, because of the objection, he would not be required to play against Lancashire 2nd—which lent more than a touch of irony to the fact that it was to Lancashire that he turned. In his first season for this deadly rival he took fourteen Yorkshire wickets for 140 runs in the Roses match, which derisive gesture led to his first England cap.

What impressive records have the Yorkshire discards, from Parkin to Illingworth via such illustrious performers as Willie Watson and J. B. Bolus. Still, proof o't pudden ... Yorkshire, since their first Championship in 1893, have been Champion County 29 times and, in 75 years up to the 1968 Championship, only appeared in the lower half of the table twice, in 1953 (13th) and 1958 (11th). So that Yorkshire, so far as its cricket is concerned, can well afford to be self-sufficient, with far greater resources than other counties and with the game as near to a religion as it is anywhere outside the West Indies.

Yorkshire, akin in relative size and fanatical local pride to Texas in the United States, spreads over four million acres which is (significantly in the minds of some God-fearing folk up there) equal to the number of letters in the Bible. Its population is around five millions, or nearly a tenth of the entire population of Great Britain. Its assets, apart from the awesomely high standards of its cricket, Soccer, Rugby League football and beer, include coal, steel, wool, a fabulous span of history—represented at either end by Bronze Age relics and Fylingdales—Delius, Priestley, the Brontes, Capt. Cook and Harold Wilson. It has, if not its own language, certainly its own vernacular and much originality of expression.

A stranger is 'an off-come'd 'un' to be treated with wary tolerance. Even natives are not expected to presume. A Yorkshire tongue-twister illustrating this reserved, if not positively suspicious attitude,

runs thus: 'Don't thee thou me, thee thou them as thou's thee.' Life
is real, life is earnest, especially upon the cricket field. Laking, with
the g permanently silent, means playing, but at Headingley or
Bramall Lane it has a sinister connotation, the implication of
'playing about' when there is serious work to be done. 'Tha's not
lakin' marbles' is as severe an admonition as an abashed Yorkshire
cricketer can expect.

In 1968 Mr John Nash, the Yorkshire secretary, reiterated the club's
inflexible qualification line thus: 'We shall continue our policy of
only playing players qualified by birth and are not concerned with the
fact that other county sides may contain an overseas star.' In fact the
'Yorkshire born only' tradition goes back to the very first match in
which a Yorkshire county team as such, took the field. It was played,
against Norfolk, on the old Hyde Park ground at Sheffield in 1833,
on September 2, 3, 4 and 5 (and there are those today who grumble
about county matches being spread over as many as three days!).
Every Yorkshire player had been, in fact, born in Sheffield, which
was the stronghold of cricket in the county in those early years.
Yorkshire gave notice of their future intentions, recording a resounding win—by 120 runs—despite the performance of the celebrated
Fuller Pilch, Norfolk-born all-rounder who later played for Kent. He
hit 10 out of 67 and 23 out of 147 and took at least 4 wickets—
probably several more, as only the name of the catcher, not the
bowler is shown in surviving score sheets of those days.

Yorkshire's most illustrious player at that time was Tom Marsden,
who scored 53 in the second innings and took several wickets. In two
single wicket matches, for the championship of England and,
incidentally, for £100, Pilch decisively beat Marsden, which necessi-
tated the first pride-swallowing exercise in Yorkshire's cricket history.
There were home and away fixtures in 1834—Norfolk handsomely
winning the first and inexplicably 'giving up' the second when within
sight of victory with Pilch on 153 not out—and in 1836, which
produced two exciting finishes, Yorkshire winning by 24 runs and
Norfolk by one wicket. Thereafter Yorkshire matches were few and
sporadic. Sussex were played in 1835, Manchester in 1844 and 1845,
Kent and Lancashire in 1849, Surrey and Lancashire in 1851,
Sheffield in 1849 and 1850. Though Sheffield figures so prominently
in the early records, Leeds was, in fact, one of the first of all Yorkshire town sides. In 1757 the Church Burgesses expended the sum of

14*s.* 6*d.* on a righteous cause thus minuted: 'Paid cricket players on Shrove Tuesday to entertain the populace and to prevent the infamous practise of throwing at cocks'.

And from the records, sparse alas!, comes this report of an occasion in 1776: 'Yesterday a cricket match was played on Chapeltown Moor by the Gentlemen of the town for 5 guineas and a dinner —married men against bachelors, which was won by the latter as there were six to come in when the game was out'. The populace, it appeared, was duly entertained, cricket and its accompanying purses and wagers, often high, proving a formidable counter-attraction to cock fighting. In 1825, when All England played 'the Rest of Yorkshire' at Sheffield (All England winning by 28 notches, the method of scoring, by nicks in a stick, until runs took over in 1836), it was recorded that: 'the whole town seemed on the alert, the roads were crowded with pedestrians and gigs, waterlows, horses etc., and, on the second day, there were from 14,000 to 20,000 persons present.' This game, like modern Test matches, was spread over five days. Though Yorkshire first appeared as a county team in 1833, it was not until 30 years later that the Yorkshire County Cricket Club came into being. On January 8th, 1863, a resolution was passed 'that a County Club be formed' to consist of 'an unlimited number of members' at a minimum subscription of 10*s.* 6*d.*

The first President was Mr T. R. Barker, a former Mayor of Sheffield and Sheffield cricketer, who nevertheless, was an 'alien', having been born at Bakewell, Derbyshire. He was, however, soon succeeded by Mr M. J. Ellison, the Treasurer, who held the two offices until his son relieved him of the Treasurership in 1894; he remained President until his death in 1897. His was the first example of the long service for which Yorkshire officials have always been noted. Lord Hawke, captain from 1883 to 1910, was President from 1898 until 1938. Since the first secretary, George Padley, was succeeded by J. B. Wostinholme in 1864 there have been only three secretaries. Mr Wostinholme held the office 39 years, F.C., later Sir Frederick Toone for 27. John Nash has carried on this increasingly onerous job with undiminished vigour and monumental tact since 1931.

To return to his predecessor but one, a mere century and a bit ago, the first years of the new county club were not without difficulty. Bradford and York, as well as Sheffield, were held to be, in effect, the representative Yorkshire teams, and in 1865 five of the new county club's best cricketers staged a 'strike'. The five who refused to play included the captain, Iddison, and a more than useful cricketer with the resoundingly Yorkshire name of Rowbotham. The results of their withdrawal of labour were that the side failed to win a match and the following year the County Committee did not make any fixtures. In 1867, however, good sense prevailed, the five 'strikers' were allowed back after apologising, and lasting harmony between Committee and cricketers was established.

Two of the most brightly shining of early Yorkshire stars now made their respective appearances, Tom Emmett, all-rounder and rare character, who became Yorkshire's captain for five years before Lord Hawke's long reign, and George Freeman, who was nominated, by none other than W.G. himself, the fastest bowler of his era. That year Yorkshire played and won seven matches. Freeman took 51 wickets averaging 7·4 runs each and Emmett 30 wickets costing only 5·2 each. There was a bit of a slump in 1868 but the season was illuminated by one historic display. John Thewlis scored the first century in Yorkshire's history and his nephew, Ephraim Lockwood, enrolled just before the match, helped him to put on 176 for the first wicket, for long a Yorkshire record. There had been some dispute as to whether or not Ephraim should fill the vacancy but Tom Emmett had said: 'Aye, Eph Lockwood is a good 'un' and that settled it. His appearance was bucolic enough to evoke metropolitan mirth but it was quickly silenced as he cut and drove with rare confidence. He was soon to become Yorkshire's finest contemporary batsman, according to Australian opinion second only to W.G. as a stroke maker. His highest innings was 208 against Kent.

In the Roses match that same year Freeman's bag was 12 wickets for 23 runs, Emmett's 8 for 24. They bowled unchanged and Lancashire were all out for 30 and 34. For Yorkshire v M.C.C. in 1872 Freeman took a match total of 10 wickets for 64 runs (Emmett had 9 for 103) and W.G. described him many years later as the fastest bowler *he* had ever played. His career was short. In only five years he played in 26 county matches and took 194 wickets costing fewer than ten runs each before business claims caused him to hand over to his fast-bowling successor, Allan Hill, who, like the greatest pair of all-rounders in Yorkshire history, Hirst and Rhodes, came from Kirkheaton.

3 Early Heroes

Tom Emmett, unlike his partner, Freeman, played for two decades and fully justified that hoary old cliché 'the life and soul of the party'. His zest was boundless, his good humour vast and infectious; his repartee enlivened many a dull day and his prowess, with both bat and ball, and especially the latter, was considerable. He was a left-hand bat and bowler, and in the latter capacity could be deadly. In 1869 he took all 10 Cambridgeshire wickets for 38 runs and, the first time Yorkshire played Surrey, he had 6 for 7. In 444 innings he aggregated 6,686 runs, averaging 15·40, and he took 1,269 wickets costing under 13 each. But it was as a 'character' that he has always been remembered, and many are the Tom Emmett stories still retold.

Who else, in all cricket, bowled a 'sostenuter'? This was his own inexplicable name for a ball which pitched on the leg stump and whipped across to remove the off bail. He claimed to have once dismissed W.G. with this one, first ball. But the doctor had ample revenge, including an innings of 150 for Gloucestershire against Yorkshire at Bramall Lane, and the highest county match score against Yorkshire, 318 not out, at Cheltenham in 1876. This prompted the immortal Emmettism; 'Grace before meat, Grace after meat and Grace all bludy day'.

Emmett once announced that he would shoot W.G. 'in the interests of the game—the pros, at any rate, would be glad!' Typical of his humour was the quip, after a number of batsmen had been dropped in a non-county match: 'There's an epidemic on this ground but, thank God, it isn't catching.' One of the most extraordinary matches in Tom's career was the Gloucester game at Sheffield in 1879. Gloucester wanted 27 runs to win with 8 wickets, including those of the three Graces, W.G., G.F. and E.M., all standing. William Bates, Yorkshire all-rounder, had a 'fancy' bet with Emmett on the result, Emmett offering 50 to 1 in shillings against his own team. When the last Gloucester man came in Emmett crept up near to the bat for a catch, which he had anticipated—and held. Had he dropped it, and news of the bet circulated, he would have been in a somewhat delicate situation, especially as he had moved without any such instruction. What he said as he cheerfully handed over the 50s. typified the Yorkshire spirit then, now and surely forever: 'Never thought about the bet—we were all so keen on winning the match.' For such a character he was singularly modest, especially when captain of Yorkshire. This was unfortunate as he sometimes failed to bowl himself when he could have been most effective.

Against Surrey, at the Oval, when he was forty years old, he tried Bates, Edmund Peate, and another great all-rounder, George Ulyett, before diffidently 'having a go' himself. He took 8 wickets for 22 runs, including a 5 for 0 spell, and Yorkshire won by 9 wickets. Fans in the crowd—and he had many, even in the deep South!—wanted to carry him back to the pavilion shoulder high. 'Nay, chaps' he said 'I have my pockets full o' brass and if you lift me up it will all roll out.' He added, when he told the story: 'I hadn't a ha'penny on me.' There was a saying about Tom: 'First a wide, then a wicket,' and, in fact, he bowled a good many wides in his career, specialising in varying both pace and direction. Lord Hawke once asked him if he had any idea how many wides he had bowled in the season. He scratched his head and replied, 'Haven't the ghost of an idea, my lord, how many?' 'Forty-five' said his lordship, whereupon Emmett demanded; 'Give me the ball, I'll soon earn talent money.' His first 'earnings', incidentally, came his way in a single-wicket match he organised as a boy for a 'purse' of twopence. He walked to the ground resplendent in white smock and clogs.

George Ulyett, like Wilfred Rhodes later, was hailed as a bowler and later proved himself a great batsman too. He was first played strictly as a bowler, and a fast one, but ended his career with 16,000 runs as well as 484 wickets to his credit. He was a cheerful character, so much so that he was known as 'Happy Jack' in days when Yorkshire cricket was, perhaps, a trifle more light-hearted than it was to become in championship chasing days. Edmund Peate was one of a succession of deadly accurate slow left-hand bowlers to whom the Yorkshire club have owed so much decade after decade, from Hodgson, in the first year of the club's existence, via Emmett, Peate, Robert Peel, Wilfred Rhodes, Roy Kilner and Hedley Verity down to Johnny Wardle a century later. Peate's career total, 819 wickets, cost only 12·55 runs apiece and his outstanding feat was a record 8 for 5 against Surrey at Holbeck in 1883.

Yorkshire's record in the first few years of the County Championship, inaugurated in 1873, was not one of spectacular success. That first year they were third behind Gloucester and Nottinghamshire. However, in 1878, the year of Australia's first tour here, they achieved the highest county score of the season, 419 v Notts, which included a century by Bates.

That summer was noteworthy for two other Yorkshire accomplishments, the skittling (by Bates and Emmett, bowling unchanged) of Sussex for 35 and 24, and the first record of a Yorkshire player, Louis Hall, carrying his bat through an innings. In 1883 Yorkshire headed the table, but, owing to the method of assessing the order of merit, Notts were named champions, having lost fewer matches. Yorkshire, in fact, had won 9, lost 2 and drawn 5 games, Notts, 4, 1 and 7 respectively—an oddly frustrating result. That year the Hon. M. B. Hawke was elected captain. He was still an undergraduate at Cambridge University but he had played for the county two years before and had, in fact, captained the side in the long vacation, taking over from Emmett.

The following year was chiefly notable for the emergence of Bobby Peel as one of the best bowlers extant. At Sheffield he disposed of Nottinghamshire virtually unaided, taking 8 wickets for 12 and 6 for 21 in two frail innings of 24 and 58. And Sheffield came into the news again when a young man from that steel city, Edward Wainwright— whose contributions to Yorkshire's future successes were to be considerable—scored 105 against the Australians in his first season.

In 1889, the year before Headingley opened its gates, Yorkshire descended to that proud county's nadir, bottom but one in the championship table, having suffered the indignity of ten defeats compared with only two victories. The next decade, however, provided a very different sort of chapter in the Yorkshire annals. Lord Hawke had by now proved himself a most resolute and authoritative captain. There had been a certain lack of discipline among the players, some of whom, it seemed, had a predilection for good Yorkshire beer which did not assist the cause of good Yorkshire cricket.

It has been said that he remarked that he had taken over a team consisting of ten drunks and a parson (the 'parson' being Louis Hall, a local Methodist preacher). This was, no doubt, a jesting exaggeration, but the fact was that the Yorkshire team, in addition to suspicions of over-conviviality, had earned the reputation, unbelievable today, of being 'too polite' to run out their opponents. His

Lordship realised that he had a tough task, to say the least of it. But by sheer strength of character, example, and the distinct advantage, at that moment in time, of aristocratic lineage, he took complete control and gradually welded a group of ruggedly individualistic characters with little sense of responsibility into a team so dedicated, loyal, and assiduous as to be among the greatest in the country. Not quite the greatest, yet. It was a long job. But as Lord Hawke was captain from 1883 until 1910 he had rather more time at his disposal than had either of those two county captains who were to show the same sort of inspired leadership between the wars and after World War Two, Brian Sellers of Yorkshire, and Stuart Surridge of Surrey.

Without a doubt the most disagreeable disciplinary task he had to perform was the dismissal of that great all-rounder, Bobby Peel who had, only the year before (1896), become the hero of the Oval Test, taking 6 Australian wickets for 23 runs to rob the tourists of what seemed certain victory. Peel enjoyed the companionship of the pot and, upon one lamentable occasion, arrived on the ground, in the modern idiom, 'stoned'. George Hirst, one of the kindest men who ever played cricket (or any other game come to that), described him in his own Yorkshire way as 'in a proper condition'. Bobby staggered in to breakfast at the hotel in which the team was staying for an away match, having, presumably, found a powerful 'hair of the dog' necessary. To save Bobby Peel's, and Yorkshire's reputation, Hirst persuaded him back to bed, even undressing him.

Then he went to see Lord Hawke and informed him that Peel had been 'taken very queer in the night' and could not play. Lord Hawke was sympathetic and promised to see poor Peel in the evening. Yorkshire went out to field, and Hirst realised, with horror, that there were twelve players, one of them Peel, in obvious disarray, ball in hand. Lord Hawke ordered him to 'leave the field at once'. But Peel insisted that he was in fine form and insisted, too, upon bowling a ball—in the direction of the sightscreen—before being led off. Lord Hawke deeply regretted that Peel had to be sacked and when they next met they were as good friends as ever.

Lord Hawke certainly was a disciplinarian and he needed to be, but the phrase for which he is inevitably remembered, 'Pray God no professional will ever captain England,' certainly did him little justice. He would not tolerate indiscipline or slackness on the field but, off it, he was the pro's friend and adviser. His was the greatest influence of all in the evolutionary process of raising the status of the professional cricketer from a position serf-like in relation to the gentleman. Autocrat he may have been, but a benevolent autocrat nevertheless.

The Peel incident upset him considerably and the loss of Peel from the team was a heavy one, to be mitigated, fortunately for Yorkshire, by the arrival on the scene of young Wilfred Rhodes, like George Hirst, from Kirkheaton, a small grey-stone village on England's backbone, the Pennines. Peel first played for Yorkshire in 1882, last in 1897, when he was forty—and he lived to be 84. For Yorkshire he scored 11,131 runs, averaging 21·28 and took 1,550 wickets costing 15·09 each. In 1895 he took 180 wickets in 1,691 overs, of which 714 were maidens, which suggests, considering the batting strength up and down the country, quite astounding accuracy. That year Hirst claimed 150 wickets. Hirst and Peel were, indeed, almost as formidable a pair as were Hirst and Rhodes in later years.

George Herbert Hirst, six years older than Wilfred Rhodes, started work at the age of ten (child labour in the 'dark, satanic mills' was not such a distant memory) for a hand loom weaver, and played cricket whenever his long hours permitted. He first played for Yorkshire in 1889 at the age of 17 but did not appear in the county side again until 1891, when he made a modest start to a wonderful career with fifteen runs and two wickets against Somerset.

In the intervening year, 1890, Yorkshire had the distinction of beating the Australians twice, by seven wickets at Sheffield and eight wickets at Bradford. It was during the season of 1892, not a very happy one for Yorkshire, that young Hirst began to reveal his vast potential. Lord Hawke liked the look of him enough to describe him as 'a young bowler with a nice action, straight and quick,' and, by the end of the season his fast and straight left-hand deliveries had brought him 99 wickets in 1,000 overs. He was not then rated highly as a batsman, going in consistently at No. 10. Yorkshire finished 6th out of 9 in the county table and recollections of the new ground at Headingley were far from joyous.

Certainly the first match had been encouraging, Derbyshire sinking peacefully and without much struggle under the onslaught of Hirst (5 wickets for 12 and 3 for 14) and Peel (3 for 26 and 5 for 7). But the two formidable London-based teams, Surrey (the Champions) and Middlesex, both beat Yorkshire at their own shiny-smart new H.Q. Yorkshire, to be sure, had won nine matches off the reel when Surrey arrived in Leeds. On a wicket soft after rain Surrey totalled 151, M.

Left: Bobby Peel, like Rhodes and Verity after him, a great left-arm spin bowler—his career so unhappily curtailed. *Below left:* Col. the Hon. Sir Stanley Jackson ('Jacker'), one of Yorkshire's greatest all-rounders and President from 1939 to 1947. *Right:* John Tunnicliffe, who hit more than 20,000 runs for Yorkshire and shared with Brown the first wicket record of 554 runs which remained unbeaten for 34 years.

Left: Lord Hawke, Captain of Yorkshire from 1883 to 1910, President from 1898 to 1938. *Below:* One of Yorkshire's finest teams in the 1890s: *Back row* (*left to right*), Turner (scorer), Wardle, Whitehead, Mr Dodsworth, Mounsey, Draper (umpire); *middle row*, Tunnicliffe, Peel, Lord Hawke, Jackson, Wainwright; *front row*, Brown, Hunter, Hirst.

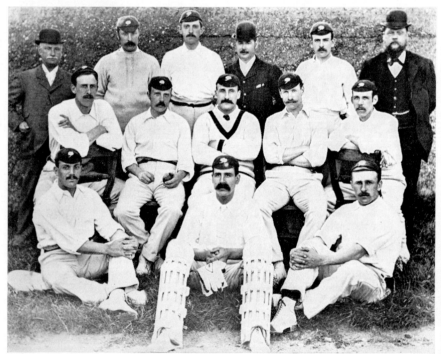

Reed's 45 proving to be the highest score in that game of changing fortunes and much excitement. Peel took seven good Surrey wickets but the bowling honours went to his chief rival, George Lohmann, who disposed of fourteen of the northerners. Surrey provided the traditional 'deathless hush' among the 15,000 spectators by losing seven wickets and then staying out there to win with just three minutes to spare. Middlesex humiliated proud Yorkshire, J. T. Hearne and fast bowler Rawlin taking all twenty wickets between them in two puny innings of 100 and 46.

From the historical point of view, 1893 was a most significant year. The unease about Sheffield's domination of the county game had reached such proportions in 1892 that decisive action was taken to end it. At that time all officers of the Yorkshire C.C.C. came from Sheffield, as did thirteen members of the Committee, with only nine from the rest of the county. The Committee was now completely reconstituted and the position of 'hub' or permanent H.Q. shifted towards Leeds, though the administrative offices were not physically transferred there until 1903. But the shift of control was manifest when the first Test match was given to Headingley in 1899, Tests against Australia having been increased from three to five. Thereafter all other Yorkshire grounds were virtually 'subsidiaries'—Bradford, Hull, Harrogate, Scarborough, Dewsbury (later replaced by Middlesbrough), even Bramall Lane, which had its last Test match in 1902.

Not only the reformation, but Yorkshire's first Championship which seemed to justify it, made '93 a year of much significance. The fact was that, new Committee or no new Committee, the team was a thoroughly sound one, especially dominant in bowling and fielding, and Lord Hawke was by now an astute and exemplary leader. Brown and Tunnicliffe, the first of Yorkshire's great opening pairs (as distinct from great openers like Hutton and Boycott, without really outstanding partners at county level) did not return spectacular averages, though they were first and second, as they were subsequently in the Yorkshire batting order for a long period. In all matches the new, young all-rounder of rare promise, F. S. Jackson, of Cambridge University, topped the batting averages with a modest 29·2 and with Brown, Tunnicliffe and Arthur Sellers, then a Keighley cricketer, exceeded 1,000 runs. 'Jacker,' as he was invariably known, showed his valiant spirit and Yorkshire determination when, in one of his earliest matches for the county, the opposing skipper, none other than W.G., brought up his field all round this comparative unknown in an attempt to speed the demolition of Yorkshire by Gloucestershire.

Lord Hawke, when a suitable moment presented itself, walked down the wicket, where he met Jacker and said to him: 'Are these old beggers trying to bustle you out?' Jacker smiled reassuringly at his captain. 'I don't know,' he said, 'but they can't.' Peel was the most successful bowler—Jacker's turn was to come—with 126 wickets, and wicket-keeper Hunter caught 58 and stumped 9 of Yorkshire's opponents. But, once again, there was humiliation at Headingley, and in the Roses match of all occasions.

Yorkshire struggled to 107, only Sellers, with 37, putting up stern resistance to fast bowler Mold. Lancashire led by 62, thanks to the brilliant Archie MacLaren with a half century despite some fine bowling by Peel. Yorkshire then collapsed in a dishevelled heap, Johnny Briggs, the England left-hand, slow-medium bowler with a two-skips-one-leap run up, taking eight of their wickets for 19 of the 53 runs which were all that the champions-to-be could muster.

Nevertheless 1893 proved to be the opening of an era of glory for Yorkshire with six Championships between then and 1902, and 146 victories compared with only 29 defeats—the other 68 matches being drawn. Hirst was now emerging as a batsman. Indeed, after he had scored 35 not out against Gloucestershire, W.G. conceded: 'I had no idea the beggar could bat as well.'

All in all, it was a summer not only of promise but of fulfilment, a summer when the sun shone day after day, so that cricket was a perpetual joy. England, at home, won the rubber against Australia for the fifth time running, and Yorkshire were acclaimed worthy champions.

This supremacy, however, could not be maintained in 1894, Surrey wrenching the title from them after beating them twice. Revenge was wrought on Somerset, which sprightly team had had the effrontery to pile up a record 542 against them the year before. In fact their journey north was scarcely necessary as they were thrashed in a single day. Sussex were demolished at Dewsbury, the demolition experts being Wainwright, who took 13 wickets for 38 runs and achieved the hat trick, and Peel. In a remarkable match at Leeds Yorkshire beat Gloucestershire due, almost entirely, to a last wicket stand of 42 by Hirst and Hunter, the ninth wicket having fallen at 19! Hunter, it would seem was, like Hirst, underrated as a batsman. In the '90s he four times helped an earlier batsman to put on more than a hundred for the last wicket—twice with Lord Hawke. Hirst was now steadily building a reputation as an all-rounder, his 100 not out v Gloucester bringing vividly back to W.G. his own prophetic words.

And, in 1895, he underlined this claim by hitting more than 700 runs as well as topping 100 wickets for the first time; topping, indeed—he took 150 wickets at an average cost of 17·06 runs, ably supporting Peel, whose average was 14·97 for 180 wickets, including fifteen in a Somerset match at Leeds. This was a formidable quick-slow combination which so often in the past proved profitable—Lancashire had one in Mold and Briggs—though it was later to be almost entirely discarded in favour of all-fast or all-spin attacks, depending, not on the known predilections and idiosyncrasies of the batsmen but upon the state of the wicket alone. With Jackson proving himself as an all-rounder, too, and with the emergence of yet another bowler, Schofield Haigh, who achieved quick fame by taking eight Australian wickets at Bradford, Yorkshire were so powerful in all departments that it is surprising that all they could achieve was third place behind Surrey and Lancashire. That year the County Championship consisted of thirteen teams, Derbyshire, Essex, Hampshire, Leicestershire and Warwickshire having been admitted. For the first time two Yorkshire batsmen reached a thousand runs in county matches—those irresistible openers Brown and Tunnicliffe.

4 All-Rounders Extraordinary

However, the Championship was Yorkshire's again in 1896, and what a season that was! Jackson was the outstanding all-rounder with a batting average in the forties. He was one of four batsmen to hit a century (117) in the record 887 amassed by Yorkshire against Warwickshire, the others being Wainwright (126) Peel (210 not out) and Lord Hawke (166, going in at number nine). Hirst, the last man but one, hit 85 including a dozen fours. Batting feats were numerous that sunny summer. Brown and Tunnicliffe scored 139 and 147 for the first wicket against Middlesex and—for the first time in the county club's history—against Leicestershire all eleven players reached double figures, in a total of 660. Five times Yorkshire scored more than 400 in an innings, twelve Yorkshire players had batting averages of more than twenty and six of them had more than 1,000 to their credit. For George Hirst it was an unforgettable year; he accomplished his first 'double', 1,112 runs and 104 wickets. From the players' point of view 1896 had a very special significance apart from these rather splendid performances—Yorkshire set an example to all other counties by giving them winter pay.

Spectacular batsmanship illuminated the summer of 1897 too. Brown and Tunnicliffe, now mature and mutually understanding partners as were Holmes and Sutcliffe years later, set up a new first wicket record, 378 out of a total of 681 against Sussex at Sheffield; it stood for a fortnight only, then Abel and Brockwell of Surrey beat it by one run. The Rev. R. S. Holmes, in *The History of Yorkshire Cricket, 1833–1903*, related an amusing aside from this feat by Yorkshire's openers. When the partnership had reached a hundred two spectators adjourned to celebrate the achievement, and announced that they would similarly celebrate every additional fifty the pair put on. When 350 appeared on the board these two devoted cronies rose, a trifle less steadily and readily it is to be assumed, and one was heard to lament: 'We shall be ruined if this goes on much longer!'

Two of the season's most exciting games took place in Yorkshire, though not at Leeds. Essex beat the northerners at Huddersfield by one run. And, at Harrogate, the immortal Gilbert Jessop gave one of his more spectacular pyrotechnic displays, hitting 101 out of 118 in just forty minutes, one towering six descending upon, and penetrating, the roof of a cab waiting outside the ground. The horse, startled out of its nosebag if not out of its wits as well, bolted and (so the legend insists) did not stop until it reached Leeds. The win of the season was achieved by Yorkshire at Derby, after a Derbyshire victory had looked fairly certain. Yorkshire, needing 154, lost Jackson and Brown for two and, subsequently, only Hirst revived hopes which flickered but feebly when the last man, Hunter joined him with sixteen runs still wanted.

The only hope for Yorkshire appeared to lie in Hunter's survival of the one ball left that over, so that Hirst could then face the bowling and attempt to hit the required runs. But, to the dismay of Hirst and all Yorkshire supporters there present, Hunter hit a single and scampered down the wicket, giving Hirst no option but to run too or lose the match. Hunter then proceeded, as if he were a well-set opener in cracking form, to hit three fours in succession, followed by a drive on the leg side which yielded the remaining runs. Whether or not the ball went over the boundary will never be known for the exultant crowd broke on to the playing area as the batsmen ran the third and match-winning run. This Jessopian display had amazed Hirst, as it had the rest of the Yorkshire team in the pavilion. What they did not know was that David Hunter had overheard a Derbyshire official, convinced that his team was about to celebrate the great event of a win over all-powerful Yorkshire, say to the dressing-room attendant: 'Bring out the champagne, Harry.' As Hunter and Hirst picked their way through the cheering throng the former was heard to observe: 'Champagne—I said I'd show 'em.'

In 1898 Yorkshire, with one of the greatest teams in its history, rose majestically from fourth place to first in the Championship table.

This, in batting order, was the team (eight of them played for England): J. T. Brown, J. Tunnicliffe, F. S. Jackson, D. Denton, E. Wainwright, Lord Hawke (capt.), G. H. Hirst, F. W. Milligan, S. Haigh, W. Rhodes, D. Hunter.

Brown and Tunnicliffe, oddly contrasting in appearance and style —Brown, craggy-chinned, short and thick-set, specialising in hooks and very late cuts, Tunnicliffe ('Long John') 6 ft. 3 in. and a powerful driver, set up a first wicket record which was to stand for 34 years, 554 runs against Derbyshire at Chesterfield. Brown's share was 300 exactly—eleven short of his highest score—Tunnicliffe's, 243. Holmes and Sutcliffe beat this record by one run in 1932.

But the event of most lasting importance in the Yorkshire annals was the appearance of twenty-year-old Wilfred Rhodes in succession to the unhappily disgraced Bobby Peel. It was said that his bowling was a major if not the main factor in Yorkshire's Championship success. At any rate in that, his first season, he took 142 wickets in county matches at an average cost of 14·6 runs each—in all first class games 154 wickets at 13·95 each. He was hailed as the most successful slow bowler of the season and *Wisden* honoured him as one of the five Cricketers of the Year. In his first appearance in first class cricket, for Yorkshire against M.C.C., Rhodes had taken six wickets, and, in the next, v. Somerset, 13, conceding only 45 runs. Jackson's all-round record was impressive, to say the least of it, 1,566 runs and 104 wickets.

In the Headingley story, the last year of the old century was one of the most important. On June 29 and 30 and July 1 the first Test match was played on that ground and Lord Hawke was largely responsible for securing it. In May the previous year he had suggested in a speech at Bedale (which figures in early Yorkshire cricket records) that Test matches should come under the control of a specially elected authority rather than a single county club. The idea was accepted and, at Lord's in July representatives of the counties agreed on a Board of Management comprising a President, five members of the M.C.C. Committee and six county representatives.

Yorkshire had one of these places. It was also decided that there should be five Test matches instead of three, that half the gross gate money should go to the visiting Australians and that the 'host' club should receive 20 per cent of the net gate, the rest going equally to the M.C.C. and all the counties. Another decision was that all professionals playing should be paid £20. The Yorkshire captain having initiated these dramatic changes it was only just that Yorkshire was awarded one of the extra Tests. Leeds was chosen as the most suitable venue, for its amenities as well as its accessibility, approach from the centre of the City by buggy, barouche, those new-fangled horseless carriages, or even on foot, being easily accomplished.

Though it was a glorious summer, rain interfered with this Test, washing out the whole of Saturday's play, which was a heavy blow to the loyal Yorkshire supporters and strangers from as far away as Manchester and even London who had gathered in large numbers in the hope of seeing England draw level. Australia were one up in the series. There had been considerable, and noisy, indignation when a not entirely impartial crowd learned that Wilfred Rhodes had been left out of England's twelve—a mass manifestation repeated many years later when Fletcher of Essex was preferred to Sharpe of Yorkshire. It was probably a bloomer, for the wicket proved to be one which would have suited the left-hander admirably. However, J. T. Brown was in the team for the only time that year (and the first time for three years), and so was F. S. Jackson. In addition to the error of leaving out Rhodes, other factors were against England's captain, A. C. MacLaren. He lost the toss to Joe Darling, who decided to bat on a soft wicket. And, at the end of the first day, Johnny Briggs was taken ill; he was out of the game for a year and the illness led to his death in 1902. He had taken three good wickets in this, the last of 33 Tests in which he had taken 118 wickets, including 15 in a match in South Africa and a hat-trick in Australia.

However, a most spectacular bowling performance was achieved by J. T. Hearne, whose hat-trick in Australia's second innings disposed of three most formidable batsmen, M. A. Noble, S. E. Gregory and Clem Hill, without a run between them. The visitors scored 172 and 224, England 220—local heroes Brown and Jackson making modest contributions of 27 and 9 respectively—and 19 for nought.

As for MacLaren's England team, so for Lord Hawke's Yorkshire side, ill-luck upset calculations. Just when another Championship seemed certain Brown was out of the game—for the whole of August—and Jackson (top of the batting averages with 47) had a shoulder injury which meant that he bowled but little. Defeat by Kent handed the title back to Surrey. It was a batsmen's year with some huge scores, notably Yorkshire's 704 (Hirst and Wainwright put on 340) and Surrey's reply, 551 for 7 (Abel and Hayward 448 between them) yet Rhodes had phenomenal success as bowler. He took more than 150 wickets, averaging 16 runs each, and achieved the bowling feat of the season, 15 Essex wickets for 56 runs. Hirst distinguished himself now as a batsman, with a record three centuries in succession, 186 v Surrey, 131 v Hants., and 138 v Notts.

With the turn of the century there came to full flower a great

partnership, unique in linking not only an understanding pair of
batsmen or a complementary pair of bowlers but both. As with so
many famous pairs, Holmes and Sutcliffe, Hobbs and Sutcliffe,
Hendren and Hearne, Gilligan and Tate, Hutton and Washbrook,
Trueman and Statham—Hirst and Rhodes were dissimilar in many
ways. Their common and enduring bonds were their mutual Kirkheaton origin, the fact that they both batted right handed and
bowled left handed, and that both played for Yorkshire and England
(in that order of priority as any Yorkshireman will concede). But
physically and characteristically they were unalike. Rhodes was
much the taller, with a lean and athletic physique, grave, even dour
on the field of battle, taciturn and subtly scheming. Hirst was
shortish, certainly below average height, chunky, broad-shouldered,
impetuous and irrepressibly gay, though he could and did, in the
modern idiom, 'blow his top' upon occasion. That they shared what
is generally called big match temperament there can be no doubt.
Whether or not it is true that, at one of the most critical moments in
Test match history Hirst said to his junior, Rhodes, 'Don't worry,
Wilf, we'll get 'em in singles,' referring to the fifteen runs still
required to beat Australia at the Oval with no batsman to come, the
fact remains that get them they did.

Rhodes was only in his fourth season in big cricket when he went
in at number eleven in as tense an atmosphere as any young cricketer
has experienced. The game had swung this way and that. Jessop had
hit a hurricane century in 75 minutes, including a five and 17 fours.
When Australia's victory seemed inevitable Hirst had performed one
of his many rescue acts, staying out there while others succumbed.
But still England were behind when the last man joined him. Rhodes
cannot recall the 'get 'em in singles' remark and thinks it improbable
but Hirst, in fact, got most of the runs in singles, including the one
which made the game a tie. And Rhodes hit the single which won the
game, continuing his run right back to the pavilion, leaving Hirst to
make his ground and battle his way through the hysterical, back-
slapping multitude, alone.

Hirst played the leading part in this dramatic stand, playing the
Australian bowling with consummate skill, but his younger partner
was to overhaul him as the years went by, in terms of runs, wickets
and England caps. Briefly recalling the records of these two cricketing
giants, Rhodes, in his long career from 1898 to 1930 hit more than
40,000 runs and took 4,188 wickets, an all-time record unlikely ever

to be beaten; he accomplished the 'double' 16 times, twice making more than 2,000 runs and taking more than 100 wickets and 23 times taking 100 wickets or more (three times 200 plus). In 58 Tests he held 58 catches, scored 2,325 runs averaging 30·19 and took 127 wickets (average 26·96).

In 1899, 1902 and even the winter of 1903–4 he batted number eleven for England; in 1909 and subsequently, number one. With Jack Hobbs he set up the first wicket record in Tests between England and Australia, 323, at Melbourne in 1911–12. George Hirst, between 1889 and 1921 (he played one match in 1929) scored nearly 37,000 runs (average 34·14) and took 2,723 wickets (average 18·75). He completed the 'double' 14 times and had the astounding record, in 1906, of scoring 2,385 runs and taking 208 wickets. In 24 Tests he scored 792 runs and took 59 wickets. Was Wilfred Rhodes the greatest of all all-rounders? Hirst thought so, though Hirst gave it as his opinion that, had F. S. Jackson been a professional he would have been the greatest cricketer of all. As it was and is Rhodes must have strong claims over all others, from 'Jacker' himself down to Keith Miller and Garfield Sobers via Frank Woolley and Wally Hammond.

I first saw him in the glorious summer of 1921 and, like so many other schoolboys squatting round the grass verge at Hove with sandwiches and ginger pop to keep us sustained, I was mesmerised. The easy, gentle run-up, the perfect, rhythmic, sideways-on action of bowler Rhodes, the unhurried confidence and supremely competent stroke play of batsman Rhodes could never be forgotten. In any case the very name was magic.

He had, indeed, figured in many a back garden 'Test', opening for England with Hobbs, followed by W.G. (lifelike with the aid of a property beard I had somehow acquired). And here he was in the flesh, tying down batsmen as he had for so many years, frustrating bowlers fast, medium or slow with equal imperturbability and giving my local hero, Joe Vine, plenty of exercise scampering round the boundary to cut 'em off and return the ball by means of an underarm throw unique in cricket and involving a lightning winding-up process. Recently I spent an afternoon with Wilfred Rhodes in the comfortable house just outside Bournemouth where now he lives with his daughter. It was an awesome and humbling, as well as nostalgic experience. For Rhodes has faced blindness with all the courage he put into his cricket and, indeed much more. He has not allowed it for one moment to quench his zest for life and for the game of which he said, when elected by the Lord's Taverners 'Cricketer of the Century', in his 91st year, 'I have always been rather fond of it'—surely the understatement of the century.

The most moving moment of all for me was when Rhodes rose (rose?—he almost leapt) from his arm chair to give me a little coaching. Holding an imaginary bat immaculately straight he moved his right foot back along the pattern of the carpet—and it was almost possible to hear the impact of the phantom ball upon the non-existent bat's middle.

'Play off the back foot' he urged—advice no doubt frequently proffered to the Harrow boys he coached with undiminished dedication in his later (in the career sense) years. 'That's the key to every stroke in cricket' he added firmly. 'I always played the fast bowlers off the back foot. You've got to give yourself more time, not go nearer and make them faster. It's common sense. They used to call me a pusher. Well, I pushed 'em to the boundary. They say it's all in how you lift the bat. Poppycock! It's how you bring it down that matters.' Upright, lean, bronzed, unbelievably nearly 92, Wilfred Rhodes, Master all-rounder, sent the ball I feel sure he could see even if I couldn't, speeding through the covers.

Was it Kortright bowling from the china cupboard end? Probably. 'Kortright seemed the fastest bowler I ever played against' Mr Rhodes declared. N. A. Knox was similar to Kortright but not so fast (Jack Hobbs once told me that Knox was the fastest bowler he ever faced)—Cotter, of Australia was 'quick, very quick indeed'. On the subject of the greatest batsman he had ever seen Wilfred Rhodes was emphatic. Bradman. 'There was nobody anywhere near him. I couldn't keep him quiet though I tried my hardest. He used his bat like a tennis racket. Mind you, it was all in the footwork.'

Bradman, one of the few 'foreigners'—that is to say, cricketers born outside Yorkshire—to be totally accepted at Headingley and all other Yorkshire grounds as if he were one of themselves, was at the start of his career; Rhodes near the end of his—the difference in their ages being just 31 years—when they met in cricketing combat. With all the pride of the Yorkshireman and the severity of the Yorkshireman robbed, Rhodes recalled that he would have had Bradman out first ball at Scarborough if he'd had a good catcher at mid-off. He made 95, the frustrated bowler thought. Going back further, Rhodes conceded that Hobbs, his one-time England opening partner, was the best bat England ever had, though he was easier to bowl to than Bradman because he played 'according to the book'. Then out popped the loyal, belligerently partisan Tyke again. Sutcliffe, Rhodes roundly asserted, never had the praise he deserved. In the 1926 Oval Test to which Rhodes himself had been recalled for his still baffling bowling, Hobbs had made 100 and Sutcliffe 161. 'On a bus going away from the ground they were all talking about Hobbs,' Rhodes related with indignation. 'A friend of mine on that bus, tired of hearing nothing but Hobbs, Hobbs, Hobbs, called out: "Wasn't there a feller named Sutcliffe playing?" Quite right, too.'

From this eventful game we went right back to Wilfred's own boyhood start as a cricketer. 'I never played on a cricket ground until I was fifteen. It was the Queen's Highway, or a bit of flat, anywhere, a sixpenny compo ball with an imitation seam and any bat we could get. Then I played for Kirkheaton seconds and worked my way up.' His father, Alfred, was captain of that team and young Wilfred owed much to his encouragement and insistence on practice on the farm where the family occupied a cottage. By 1900 Wilfred Rhodes was a seasoned cricketer far beyond his 23 years.

Indeed, though the Yorkshire team that year was one of the most powerful in the county's history, awesomely efficient in all departments, Rhodes was outstanding. He took more wickets, 261, than in any other season—more, indeed, than any other Yorkshire bowler before or since. Hirst, on the other hand, had a comparatively poor season as a bowler, shining, instead, as a batsman with nearly 2,000 runs and an average over 40. As he also took 62 wickets and Rhodes scored 655 runs the pair's share in the county's resounding success was not exactly inconsiderable.

Schofield Haigh to a large extent made up for Hirst's temporary loss of bowling form, taking 145 wickets at a very economical price, 14 runs each. All three had to pull out that little extra in the absence, fighting in the Boer war, of Capt. the Hon. F. S. Jackson who was serving in (of all regiments!) the Royal Lancasters. Frank Milligan, useful batsman and change bowler, also served in South Africa where, that year, he died, to the great sorrow of the Yorkshire team of which he had been a most popular member.

But Yorkshire's resources were such during that period—as they have been often enough since without any outside help—that main interest among the other counties lay in the answer to the question: 'Who will be runners-up?' In the first game of the 1900 season

Yorkshire scored a puny 99—and won by an innings. All that
Worcestershire could scrape together were totals of 43 and 51.
Thereafter Yorkshire were the masters though not as overwhelm-
ingly, unchallengeably the masters as in the following year. Now
Hirst supplanted Haigh, who was suffering from knee trouble, and
a tremendous power in the attack he soon proved to be. He was very
fast and such was his stamina that he was virtually tireless. No bowler
in the country could make the ball swerve in the air as he did and few
batsmen had much relish in facing him.

   S. M. J. Woods, the immortal Sammy, summed up for them all
thus: 'How the devil can you play a ball that comes at you like a
hard throw-in from cover point?' With Rhodes nagging away at the
other end, impassive, imperturbably probing each batsman's weak-
nesses, the pair were menacing indeed. All Yorkshire's batsmen made
runs that glorious season, Frank Mitchell emerging as the most
successful with an aggregate of 1,674, averaging 49 per innings. And
John Brown reaped a record (up to then) benefit of £2,300. It was a
fine weekend and Lancashire were the visitors. So that on August
Bank Holiday such crowds descended upon the Headingley ground
that improvisation was necessary. Officials humanely decided that it
would be ungenerous as well as unwise to turn away spectators. So
the boundaries were shortened and, after some delay, 30,000 were
packed into the ground in such a way that all could see the play.
How any county's administrators (and certainly any beneficiary)
would welcome such an attendance today! Batsmen were on top most
of the game, especially Frank Mitchell, a rugby player from South
Africa born, of course, in Yorkshire, and, for the opposition, Archie
MacLaren. Very properly, considering the occasion, Yorkshire were
victorious.

5 The Era of 'Jacker'

When Yorkshire were not demolishing their opponents with almost unseemly haste they were quite capable of putting up the shutters to ensure against defeat—as when the team, to the entire county's consternation, totalled only 92 in reply to 560 by Fry-and-Ranji-resplendent Sussex. Brown and Tunnicliffe dug in deeper than any of the embryo cricketers with their spades on nearby Brighton beach, and played out three hours of time for 107 runs to save the day. Twenty out of twenty-seven matches were decisively won, six drawn and only one lost—to Somerset at Leeds. This was, without question, the game of the year, and one of the most remarkable in cricket history. Somerset were bowled out for 87 and, when Yorkshire had built a sound and solid 325, the only result appeared to be an innings victory for the champions. But the lads oop from Zummerzet, though they had taken the precaution of laying on alternative travel arrangements for the second day just in case, were never easily daunted. Gaily and contemptuously they slogged the most relentlessly efficient attack in England, impudently keeping the scoring rate scampering along at more than eighty r.p.h. Lionel Palairet, the elegant stroke maker and hard hitter who had partaken in the record first wicket stand against Yorkshire in 1892, proceeded to demonstrate that this was no fluke with a majestic innings of 173, Len Braund hit 107 and Phillips 122.

Somerset's total reached 630. For once downcast, Yorkshire on a worn wicket could only manage 113, and Somerset triumphed by 279 runs—a wider margin, even, than their deficit on the first innings. Leeds was virtually in mourning. Voices were muffled, pints were consolatory rather than celebratory. That graceful writer the late, alas, A. A. Thomson related (in *Hirst and Rhodes*) the story of the dishevelled Tyke, apparently an escaped prisoner of war, who crawled up to Capt Jackson, who was inspecting his lines, saluted and asked: 'Excuse me, sir, how did Yorkshire get on again' Somerset?' When Jackson told him the awful news he shuffled away. 'Here,

where are you off to?' asked Jackson. 'I'm off back to the Boers,'
replied the scarecrow figure. Rapidly turning this dismal page in the
Yorkshire annals, there was also recorded that season the county
championship's lowest score, 13, reached with difficulty by, of all
teams, those pioneers and early champions, Nottinghamshire.
Rhodes took 6 wickets for 4 runs in 7·5 overs, Haigh 4 for 8 in 7 overs.

Jacker was back in 1902, a year remarkable not only for the
sustained lustre of Yorkshire, again beaten only by Somerset, but for
much drama, including a titanic struggle with the Australians, who
won the rubber by three runs only, and the dismissal of that formidable side twice for under 40. The chief executioner was George
Herbert Hirst. England's team in the first Test match, reputed to be
the strongest ever fielded up to then, compiled 376, with Rhodes 38
not out at number eleven. The light was poor but not so bad that
anyone present could have foreseen the debacle to come. In eleven
overs each, Rhodes and Hirst shot the powerful Australian side out
for 36 runs, half of them made by the indomitable Victor Trumper.
Rhodes took 7 wickets for 17 runs, Hirst 3 for 15. The weather
robbed England of a victory as certain as any could be.

After that haunting experience the Australians journeyed to Leeds
where, on a truly treacherous Headingley pitch (it was an atrocious
summer to challenge in misery, say, 1958), they played Yorkshire,
which was over optimistically regarded as a less daunting task than
playing England. Victor Trumper, on such a wicket, played one of
the best innings in his illustrious career. It reached only 38 but was
generally held to be the equivalent of a century or even a double
century on a good batting wicket. The Australians struggled to 131,
which was creditable enough and more, by 24, than Yorkshire
could achieve. The Australians then resumed their siege against a
merciless attack—with modified success until Trumper was bowled
by a ball which Hirst regarded as the best he bowled in all his life.

At the other end was F. S. Jackson, bowling his fast-medium
straight deliveries with deadly accuracy. The pair proved unplayable.
The score was transformed in a few minutes from 20 for 3 to 23 all
out. After Trumper, Hirst bowled Noble and Armstrong, then
Jackson polished off the remainder, taking 3 wickets in 5 balls. Hirst
had taken 5 for 9 and Jackson 5 for 12. Yorkshire won, but only just,
for 48 runs constituted a difficult target in those conditions. And no
Test match victors ever received more thunderous approbation than
did the conquering county men that day. This jubilation turned to

sour wrath when Hirst was left out of the Manchester Test and Fred
Tate of Sussex (whose career tragedy was the dropped catch which
was said to have lost the game for England) was played. 'It were
thrown away' was the verdict of the West Riding.

Yorkshire descended from the top to third place in 1903—
Middlesex were champions with Sussex runners-up—due to a series
of set-backs early in the season. Irving Washington, a resolute bat
who had been responsible for the winning hit against Australia in
that memorable Headingley game the year before, was taken ill.
Hirst had trouble with a calf muscle, Tunnicliffe split his hand, T. L.
Taylor, leading batsman the year before was abroad, Jackson could
only play occasionally and Lord Hawke was ill part of the season.
Ernest Smith, a reliable batsman, as a schoolmaster could only play
in the latter part of the programme.

But Hirst was now demonstrably one of the greatest all-rounders
in the country. Indeed he was repeatedly referred to that year (Hirst's
year, as 1905 was Jackson's year) as 'the world's greatest all-rounder'
which was a trifle mortifying for his incredibly consistent 'twin',
Rhodes, whose record was scarcely less lustrous (193 wickets, average
14·57 and 1,137 runs, average 27·07, compared with Hirst's 128
wickets, average 14·94 and 1,844 runs, average 47·28). Had Yorkshire's fielding been better—for once it fell far below its normally
exemplary standard—Hirst might well have improved on this record.
The highlight of season 1904, from Yorkshire's point of view
generally and Hirst's particularly, was the Roses match at Headingley, set aside for Hirst's benefit. And George Herbert Hirst, after a
dozen years of sterling service with his native county, was not only
the star attraction but the star performer. MacLaren won the toss
and put Yorkshire in to bat. A huge crowd, tense and with deepening
gloom, saw five wickets fall for far too few runs. Hirst had been
given the sort of reception usually reserved for conquering heroes and
he was still in the middle when it was the turn of schoolmaster
Ernest Smith to bat.

The pair proceeded to give Lancashire 'the stick' so that the mood
at Headingley was transformed from dejection to jubilation. The sun
shone, the weather was perfect—as it was for all three days—and it
was (through a generous change of dates by Lancashire) Bank
Holiday weekend. When Hirst returned to the pavilion the ovation
could have been heard in Kirkheaton. Every one of the 31,826
spectators upon the ground rose to acclaim him in a warmly

cacophonous tribute which can rarely have been equalled. (The total 3-days attendance was 78,792, enough to bring tears to the eyes of present day club secretaries.) Smith and Lord Hawke pushed the score along, still at a brisk pace, adding 130, so that it reached a very respectable 403. Hirst had not by any means finished his benefit celebrations. In his first over he bowled the illustrious Spooner (who, with MacLaren had set up a Lancashire first wicket record of 368 the year before) and in his third over took the wickets of those other two batsmen forming the great Lancashire triumvirate of those days, MacLaren himself, and J. T. Tyldesley. Hirst's benefit fund reached £3,703, a new record by a big margin, and a fair fortune in those days when a pound was a sovereign and went a long, long way.

It stood as a record for twenty-one years, until Roy Kilner received £4,016 in 1925. Lancashire had gone to Headingley with an unbeaten record and, thanks to a brilliant second innings century by Johnny Tyldesley, they took it away with them, though they had to be content with a draw. And Yorkshire had to be content with second place behind them in the county championship.

Hirst finished a glorious season in a blaze of glory. He reached the massive aggregate of 2,501 runs averaging 54·36, and took 132 wickets costing 21·09 runs each. This was the first time any Yorkshire player had exceeded 2,000 runs and 100 wickets and, in the matter of runs total, has never been beaten. Rhodes accomplished a similar double in 1909 and 1911, and, though he took nine more wickets than Hirst in the former year, he never reached 2,500 runs in a season, nor was his batting average ever as high as Hirst's in Hirst's year. David Denton passed a rare milestone for a wicketkeeper, a thousand wickets in first-class cricket.

The year 1905 belonged to F. S. Jackson and, under his captaincy, to England, too. Briefly, Jackson's psychological contribution to England's triumph over Australia was to win the toss in all five Tests (so that Darling, the Australian captain, in mock despair said to him, 'What the use of tossing with you, Jacker, I might just as well give you the first innings.').

His more practical contributions were to win the only Test that was finished and to head England's Batting *and* Bowling averages with 1,492 runs (average 70·28) and 13 wickets (15·46 apiece). Moreover, Jackson had the extreme satisfaction of scoring a century on his own home ground of Headingley at a time when runs were, to say the least of it, badly needed. Four wickets were down for 64 runs when Jackson and Hirst put a stop to the rot—how many, many times Hirst had to come to the rescue—almost doubling the score before Hirst was caught by Trumper. Bosanquet, of googly fame, was next and there was little batting to come thereafter. Jackson, who had started with considerable caution, now increased the pace, scoring twice as fast as 'Bose', who, nevertheless helped him to push the score to 192. Wicket-keeper Lilley and Haigh helped to put on 31 and 50 and England were all out for 301 just before the scheduled close of play. Jackson was not out 144 and 244 of England's runs had been scored while he was at the wicket. It was, if not the best, one of the best displays of determined, sound and virtually chanceless batting he ever gave—and there were many good ones. Almost all his runs were scored safely 'along the carpet', from cuts and drives, particularly drives of rare power on the on side.

He hit eighteen fours. Rhodes was out of the side with an injured finger (to the dismay of the Leeds crowd) and a newcomer, Warren of Derbyshire, bowling very fast in his first—and last—Test match was the most successful bowler with 5 wickets for 57 runs in Australia's first innings of 195, and 1 for 56 in the second, 224 for 7. Jackson declared England's second innings at 295 for 5 after Tyldesley, with a duck in the first innings, had scored exactly 100. Armstrong took all 5 wickets—plus 2 in the first knock. There was a curious parallel with the Nottingham Test, which England had won by 213 runs. Jackson declared at precisely the same time and left the Australians exactly the same number of runs to get in both matches. At Headingley, however, it didn't work, Armstrong, with 32 (after 66 in the first innings) and Noble, with 62, enabling Australia to hang on and make a draw of it. Colin Blythe, Kent's celebrated left-arm bowler, took three good wickets but the bowlers were unable to clinch the issue.

Jackson was a joyous cricketer, enormously zestful as batsman, bowler and fielder. Cricket came first always, his own performances being merely a means to the end of a good game well fought. It was typical of him that he declared in the victorious first Test when he was 82 not out and racing to his century.

My own personal recollection of him is vivid—a lean, lithe, handsome man, his moustache by then grey but as neatly military as ever, demonstrating to me, in his study in London's Pont Street (later to be bombed by that non-cricketing criminal lunatic Adolf Hitler) how he would have dealt with the so-called (by Australians) body-line, or

(by us) leg-theory bowling. With a malacca cane he swept imaginary
bumpers of lethal potential off the tip of his aristocratic nose in the
general direction of Buckingham Palace. Sir Stanley Jackson, then a
Test Selector, and soon afterwards Chairman of the Selection Committee, had not lost a shred of that vast enthusiasm for the game he
adorned for too short a time. A full and busy public life had meant
that he had not been able to give nearly as much time to cricket as his
hosts of fervent admirers would have liked. The 1905 season was his
last on a full-time basis; he played a few times only in 1906 and 1907,
and his twenty Tests were all home games and all against Australia,
from whose bowlers he took 1,415 runs at an average of nearly 49 per
innings. He also captured 33 of their wickets for 24 runs each. In all
matches his totals were 16,251 runs, average 33, and 834 wickets,
average 19. A feat he recalled, understandably with some relish,
distinguished the Gentlemen v Players match in 1894. He and his
former Cambridge University captain, Sammy Woods, bowled
unchanged in both innings, Jackson taking 13 wickets for 77 runs.
He also hit 63, the highest score.

Sir Stanley entered Parliament as M.P. for Howdenshire, Yorkshire, and, soon after his introduction, met Winston Churchill, who
had been his fag at Harrow. Lloyd George, who was present at this
historic meeting, greeted him with: 'I have been looking all my life
for the fellow who gave Winston Churchill a hiding at school!'
Jackson became Secretary to the War Office and also Chairman of
the Unionist (Conservative) Party organisation. But he never forsook
cricket. He became President of the M.C.C. and, after Lord Hawke,
President of Yorkshire.

Returning briefly to 1905, Yorkshire had to take the field in a
number of matches without their stars. Jackson was engaged in all
five Tests, Rhodes in four, Denton and Haigh in one each. Lord
Hawke had, in a burst of patriotic fervour, declared that it must be
'England first and the rest nowhere.' Yet Yorkshire did win the
Championship, for the seventh time since its inception, the fourth in
six years. In those six years the team had won 89 games out of 164
played, and lost only twelve.

After losing to Lancashire, Derbyshire and Kent early in the
season, the county had an unbeaten run, ending the season fittingly by
beating the Rest of England. The outstanding individual feat of the
year was Hirst's mammoth score off the Leicestershire bowlers.
Leicester had hit 419, C. J. B. Wood playing through the entire

innings for 160, and Yorkshire looked to be in distinct peril at 74 for 5. Hirst, at number five, having survived an appeal for l.b.w. before he had scored, hit with supreme confidence all round the wicket. When he was last out after seven hours at the crease his own score was 341 out of Yorkshire's 515. This remained the highest individual score by a Yorkshireman until Hutton's 364 against Australia 33 years later. Wood spent much of the match on the field, but, this was restful compared with his unique feat in the same match six years later. He was then upon the field while every ball of the match was bowled, carrying his bat right through both innings for 107 not out and 117 not out—a performance without parallel.

But Hirst's greatest all-round triumph, unique in many respects and unlikely ever to be beaten, was achieved in 1906, a year remarkable also for a thrilling end to the championship fight, Yorkshire losing it by one run.

Hirst's figures were: batting—2,385 runs in 58 innings, average 45·86; bowling—208 wickets in 1,306 overs, average 16·50. The sheer vigour of the man taxes the imagination. For here was, not a slow bowler who strolled up to the wicket to wheel over a beguiling arm, but a fast bowler with an urgent, bounding run and a swiftly whirling arm, the entire action and delivery involving a vast, though seemingly inexhaustible expenditure of energy. At the same time, here was a batsman capable of fierce and sustained aggression—or dogged, hour after hour sticking it out. He was, in addition, the finest mid-off playing—perhaps the best ever—for the off drive was a favourite shot then with some mighty powerful exponents including R. E. Foster, Reggie Spooner and Lionel Palairet.

You may search the records with as much diligence as you like in a vain attempt to find a parallel to Hirst's performance in the last county game of that wearying season. Against Somerset he made 111 and 117 not out and took 6 wickets for 70 runs followed by 5 for 45. Clearly he was not exaggerating when he replied to the inevitable question, 'Do you think your records will ever be beaten?' with: 'I don't know, but whoever does will be very tired.' The match which cost the Championship immediately preceded the Somerset game.

Gloucestershire led on the first inning by five runs and Yorkshire eventually needed 234 runs to win. Rhodes hit 52, the amateur T. L. Taylor, 41, and Horace Rudston 40—at which point he hit his wicket trying to square cut the Gloucester captain, hurricane batsman Jessop, who had boldly put himself on. Yorkshire bowler Ringrose was last man and, with one run needed for a tie, Jessop bowled him a loose one. Wicket-keeper Board hurled himself sideways, goalkeeper-like, to bring off a truly spectacular save. Two balls later Ringrose was out l.b.w. The narrowest possible defeat allowed Kent to nose ahead to the Championship, of which they were not unworthy. *Wisden* noted: 'The colt, Woolley deserves more than passing notice'. And, illustrating the rigidly insular Yorkshire attitude, another quote is worth including. Commenting on the appearance of Cecil Parkin and his subsequent 'deportation', A. W. Pullin ('Old Ebor') in his invaluable *Yorkshire Cricket 1903–1923* wrote: 'The Yorkshire Committee and Lord Hawke did not require to be told their duty in the matter.'

Headingley's highlight in 1907, without a doubt, was the Test match against South Africa, won by England after many dramatic changes of fortune and scampers to the pavilion to shelter from the merciless and ever-returning rain.

6   End of an Epoch

C. B. Fry selected the 1907 Leeds Test v South Africa as 'the game of a lifetime' when asked for his choice by my old friend the late—and most widely lamented—Denzil Batchelor. Denzil included it in his book with that title, describing it as 'the marvellous up-and-down, in-and-out game' and concluding: 'There never was another wet-wicket Test in England fraught with such electrifying drama.' South Africa had sent us a strong side, particularly in bowling and, more particularly, in googly bowling, with such leading exponents as R. O. Schwarz and A. E. Vogler—who had studied its inventor, Bosanquet, during some appearances in the Middlesex side. These two opened the bowling to Fry and Tom Hayward after rain had fallen on the wicket. Only nine runs had been scored when Vogler yorked Fry and, thereafter, the struggle for survival became more and more tense on a wicket which became a soggy demon. Hayward was out at 24 and only Hirst, grimly aware that every man, woman and child upon the ground expected him to save the day, made the bowling look as if it were just playable. Jessop, hitter extraordinary, was almost run out first ball, then edged the second into the wicket-keeper's hands off Faulkner. England were all out for 76 and Faulkner, whose length had been near faultless, spin disconcerting and 'wrong'un' unspottable, was the most successful bowler with 6 wickets for 17.

South Africa fared little better, the narrow escapes of the opening pair eliciting indelicate gasps and groans from the normally phlegmatic crowd. Their anguished disgust was undisguised when the slippery ball was dropped by Arnold—off their idol, Hirst. However, he made amends by catching Nourse off Blythe when South Africa were showing ominous signs of conquering the keen bowling, the hostile pitch and the atrocious weather. In such circumstances their first innings lead of 34 was daunting. But Fry was not to be sent packing a second time. He and J. T. Tyldesley defied the slings and arrows and even storms, Faulkner, Schwarz and Vogler, to build up the only respectable total of this hard-fought match, 162. Fry's share was 54, Tyldesley's 30.

At the start of the third day, with England 111 for 4, a draw looked
the most likely result, especially after the players had fled from the
rain no fewer than six times. But the pitch, and Colin Blythe, the
slight, frail but indomitable left-hand spinner from Kent, who was to
lose his life so soon afterwards in the First World War, once more
wrought a transformation. With South Africa 3 for 2 wickets,
England's hopes began to soar again. Blythe, indeed, bowled with
magnificent accuracy and guile. Moreover he could grip the wet ball,
no easy accomplishment. It was clear that he was cast as man of the
match. If he failed South Africa could win.

Fry said afterwards that half a dozen 'moderate' overs from Blythe
would have given them the match. There were no moderate overs,
not even loose balls. Blythe lured batsman after batsman to destruction, all his seven wickets except one being catches for which he had
bowled with deadly deliberation. South Africa were all out for 75,
England had won by 53 runs, a volcanic peak of tension subsided and
Blythe received the ovation due to the hero of the day and the
match. In the two innings he had bowled 38·1 overs and taken 15
wickets for 99 runs.

Yorkshire, with a team less well balanced than in the golden years,
lost the Championship, which went, deservedly, to Nottinghamshire.
By way of compensation, Lancashire were decisively beaten at
Headingley in spite of a good opening stand by MacLaren and
Spooner. Rhodes was, as so often before and after, a determining
factor with both bat and ball. Jackson, in his only appearance that
year, scored 35 of the 133 runs wanted for victory, Tunnicliffe and
Denton nonchalantly securing the rest. Oddly, after a patchwork
performance that year, in the season following Yorkshire were as
good as ever they had been, if not rather better—Lord Hawke
nominated the 1908 team his favourite of all those he had skippered.
At any rate it was unbeaten, as in 1900, with 16 matches won and 12
drawn.

A phenomenon seared across the cricketing scene in 1908, and
disappeared almost as swiftly as a shooting star—J. T. Newstead,
forcing bat and right-arm, fast-medium, viciously off-breaking
bowler of considerable hostility at his short-lived peak. Although he
was regarded then as a 'discovery' he had, in fact, been given a trial
as a batsman for the Yorkshire team in 1903. And in August the
previous year he had bowled himself into the *Year Book's* 'Exceptional Bits of Bowling' pages (where he may still be found in the

current edition) with 7 Leicestershire wickets for 10 runs. Now he blossomed into an all-rounder but particularly into a bowler who would almost certainly have played for England had there been any Test matches that year. Noteworthy feats included 7 wickets for 68 and 100 not out against Nottinghamshire. His bowling was an important factor in the county's success, especially as Haigh was a spectator for some weeks with a broken spinning finger. When he finished the season with 131 wickets averaging under 16 to his credit —and with a 25 batting average by way of bonus—a lustrous future was predicted, though he was 28. But the following year he seemed to have lost his length as well as his fire and thereafter his appearances became rarer until he settled for League cricket.

Apart from the unfulfilled promise of Newstead and some hope-raising performances by a 22-year-old Leeds cricketer named Hardisty, 1908 was an unspectacular season, good bowling and fielding keeping Yorkshire at the top. In July a very proper tribute was paid to Lord Hawke for having completed twenty-five years as captain of the Yorkshire XI. At Headingley in the match against that ancient enemy, Notts., the Earl of Wharncliffe presented him with six works of art, chosen by Lord Hawke himself and bought with £1,000 raised by the County Club and £824 collected in subscriptions to the 'Tyke Fund' initiated by the *Yorkshire Evening Post*. The 'Tyke', which has been a friendly if not always welcome nickname for a Yorkshireman wherever he is encountered by 'foreigners' from other counties, was created by a cartoonist on that estimable news-paper—which seems to demonstrate the power of the Press. Lord Wharncliffe assured the assembly that Lord Hawke had not adopted the methods of the martinet but, 'by firmness, by unvarying courtesy, by kindness, by a sincere love of the game, had brought Yorkshire cricket to the highest degree of efficiency and had also earned the confidence and affection of the men'. Lord Hawke, in reply, said that he had been supported by 'some of the greatest cricketers and some of the most charming fellows who had ever stepped out on a cricket field' and there had been 'no playing for self'.

His Lordship, with becoming diffidence, said that he did not know how to reply to the nice things that had been said about him. A voice from somewhere in that large and appreciative gathering suggested: 'Get a good score and tha'll be alright.' Lord Hawke thereupon contributed two modest not out innings of 17 and 8 to help his side to victory by 140 runs.

A poor season climatically and, to some extent from the point of view of Yorkshire's, and England's prestige, was to follow in 1909. The county slumped to third place in the Championship, England lost the rubber to Australia, and even Hirst had an in-and-out record suggesting (quite wrongly as it turned out) that he was nearing the end of his unique powers. Certainly he had flashes of the old brilliance, notably in the only Test won by England, due in large measure, to his 4 wickets for 28 runs and 5 for 58. And again, at Headingley, when he took 7 Middlesex wickets for 95 runs, 'old' David Hunter, in his 21st season with Yorkshire, snapping up six catches behind the wicket in one innings—an exhibition of agility to belie his 49 years. For Yorkshire, the dismal depths were plumbed at the Oval when Surrey, having led by 50 in the first innings and then been summarily dismissed by Hirst (7 for 27) for 62, annihilated the Champions, reversing those figures. On a horrific wicket, 'Razor' Smith took 5 for 12 and Rushby 5 for 9. Yorkshire, 26 for 6, lost their last four wickets without a run being added. They have not, so far, succeeded in under-cutting that dolorous record.

The Leeds Test was hardly a happy occasion either. This contest forever belongs to Charlie Macartney—in the unusual role of bowler. England looked like comfortably beating Australia's first innings total of 188 but, from 130 for 2, the side collapsed and finished the innings six runs short. Incomparable Barnes, tall, right hand, fast-medium and dead cunning, found the wicket as helpful as had dapper, slow, left hand Macartney. With Australia 127 for 7 matters appeared to be veering our way but Macartney now assumed the role for which he was to be respectfully remembered by posterity, that of the compleat batsman. He was not exactly entertaining on this occasion, as he was to be on the same ground a dozen years later ('the Governor-General', as he was commonly known, came to relish the Headingley ground as did Don Bradman and Arthur Morris in later years) but his stubborn defence enabled Australia to set England 214 to win. Macartney then demonstrated the impossibility of this task, emerging with a match record of 11 wickets for 85 runs.

If the doings of 1909 had occasioned no widespread Yorkshire rejoicing, those of 1910 wrought a more positive reaction—downright depression! Yorkshire plummeted to eighth in the Championship table. The depth of Yorkshire gloom was hardly justified by the team's performances, for, after all, ten Championship matches were won and only seven lost—eight in all games, which totalled thirty-two. But so high were, are, and always will be the sights of Yorkshire folk that disappointment was manifest, especially when their team was robbed of victory by violent rain in the Roses match at Headingley. Lancashire had led by 77 on the first innings but, by Gow, sir, how George Herbert skittled 'em in the second. Lancashire were all out for 61 and this was the analysis of this rejuvenated (after that temporary fading the year before), nearly 39-year-old fast bowler:

O	M	R	W
13·2	2	23	9

Eight Lancastrians had been clean bowled; twice the hat-trick had been 'on' but had just eluded Hirst as did, then and on three other occasions, the coveted 'all ten'. Yorkshire were forty for one, needing fewer than a hundred, when the robbery took place. Despite the frustration, Yorkshire wit gleamed through. When Hirst was presented with the ball for his feat, Schofield Haigh, who had taken that other wicket, remarked: 'Nay, George, it's half for thee and half for me—*we* got the wickets.'

Hirst was back at the top if Yorkshire were not. In a grandstand finish at Lord's Yorkshire beat Middlesex by two wickets, the winning hit coming off the last ball but one of the last over of the game—and it was Hirst's masterly 137 which made this spectacular victory possible. Rhodes it was who beat Surrey with an undefeated 88 on a truly treacherous pitch—one of the best innings of his career—and he took eleven wickets in the match for seventy-two runs. David Hunter gave place to Arthur Dolphin, only the fifth Yorkshire wicketkeeper in sixty years—the other three being Ned Stephenson, George Pinder and Joe Hunter.

And now, at last, it was Lord Hawke's turn. After the season's end, in November, he tendered his resignation, a wrench indeed after twenty-eight years as captain. His share of responsibility for Yorkshire's tremendous reputation and awesome example had been incalculable, his own performances by no means inconsiderable. Though never one of the 'greats' as a cricketer, in the thirty years since he had first played for the county he had scored more than 16,000 runs, averaging more than 20 an innings, had been not out exactly a hundred times, and had hit 13 centuries.

Mr. E. J. (later Sir Everard) Radcliffe took over from Lord Hawke, for whom he had already deputised, and was faced with an unenviable task, with old players departing and new ones to be moulded in the

Yorkshire way if the team was to recapture its former glory. New-comers included Major (his Christian name, not his rank) Booth, and Alonzo Drake, players of great promise, neither of whom survived the First World War. But Hirst and Rhodes were still there and, if Yorkshire failed to hoist themselves more than one rung up the ladder, there were some estimable collective as well as individual performances.

Hirst had fully recovered his command of the ball, demonstrating the fact with such 'routine' performances as 6 wickets for 26 runs against Derbyshire and 6 for 34 against Sussex, both on his native heath. In the return Sussex fixture at Hastings, Hirst switched roles and hit the not very formidable Sussex bowling to all parts of that attractive seaside ground, scoring 218, the third highest innings in his career, at such speed and with such undiminished vigour as to put new heart into those who feared that he was 'too old at forty'. The result was the most resounding victory for the invaders since the Normans visited the district. Yorkshire amassed 522 runs for the loss of 7 wickets, and won by an innings. As if to underline the fact that he was still one of the world's greatest all-rounders, George Herbert Hirst, having taken 9 Worcestershire wickets for 41 runs, to bundle out one of the strongest batting sides among the counties, with scarcely a breather went to the crease, crisply and swiftly scoring a century. The latter feat was much less spectacular than the former, for this was a truly plumb wicket and, indeed, it yielded nearly 1,000 runs for 20 more wickets before Yorkshire (or Hirst) won with all second innings wickets intact.

Booth, in the first innings, recorded his first century for Yorkshire, a quite superb 210, his square cutting and off-driving proclaiming that here was a new star indeed. Drake gave a splendid all-round display in the Lancashire battle, helping Hirst to put on 193 runs and then taking 6 wickets for 57. It was not surprising, therefore, that Booth and Drake were described as 'the most valuable recruits Yorkshire have brought forward for some considerable time.'

Wilfred Rhodes, following tradition, selected the Lancashire match for his benefit—at Sheffield that year, the venue being dictated by a rota system. Gates, it had been said with some truth, had not been good at Leeds but perhaps the older ground, Bramall Lane, would draw the crowds. Unhappily the gates were not very good there either. The county's comparatively lowly position may have had something to do with it for Yorkshire folk couldn't stomach their team being among the 'also ran'. However, subscriptions for the greatest of all all-rounders were generous and the total reached £2,202 1s. 10d., a satisfactory nest-egg in those days. At the end of the season Mr Radcliffe handed over the captaincy to Sir Archibald White, who had played a number of times for the county with moderate batting success.

With a team of veterans and quickly maturing young players forming a much better balanced combination, he was able to lead Yorkshire to their ninth Championship. In twenty years Yorkshire had won 280 out of 515 championship matches, losing only 65, a record far superior to that of all other counties, the nearest being the old arch enemy, Lancashire. It was a wet summer with many blank days, which makes the performances of David Denton, now one of the veterans at 38, all the more creditable. He scored 2,127 runs, more than any other English batsman including Jack Hobbs, whose aggregate was 2,042. Only these two passed the 2,000 mark and Yorkshiremen were mightily indignant that Denton was not chosen for any of the six Tests in the not very successful triangular tournament involving Australia and South Africa.

Rhodes, B. B. Wilson and Hirst all topped 1,000 runs but the gap between this trio and Denton was wide. Rhodes, however, played in all the Test matches. Hirst once more accomplished the double, the only other cricketers to do so being Frank Woolley, Frank Tarrant, the Australian playing for Middlesex, J. H. King, Albert Relf and H. L. Simms. Schofield Haigh, aged 41, was the most successful bowler, with 125 wickets and a remarkable analysis in the county's game against the Australians, 5 for 22 and 6 for 14. The second Test against South Africa, lamentably weak compared with the 1907 side, was played at Headingley and, much to the dismay of the spectators, Rhodes for once failed. Opening with Hobbs, who was in tremendous form, he was out for 7 (the position was reversed in the Australian Test at Manchester when Hobbs was out for 4 and Rhodes, 'digging out of the slush', scored 92, a noble knock in the circumstances). In the second innings Rhodes was out for 10 and he failed to take a wicket.

Yorkshire appeared to be an even better team in 1913 than in 1912 and, in fact, won three more matches. But Kent just headed them in the County Championship. It was a memorable summer, often warm and sunny, so that gates were gratifyingly big.

That little war cloud on the horizon which was to darken the sky

so soon, was still 'no bigger than a man's hand', and the mood of
Britain was—perhaps because there was uncertainty in the air—to
enjoy life in general and our summer pursuits in particular. While
pretty girls were hiding their curves beneath all-concealing below-the-
knee bathing costumes and their curls beneath caps like pudden'
covers as they stepped coyly from bathing machines at Bridlington
and Scarborough, the match of the season was being enacted before a
large and eager crowd at Headingley. It was the August Bank
Holiday weekend, just a year before England was at war with the
Kaiser's Germany, and Yorkshire was locked in battle with Lancashire—one of the classic battles in that endless war. Not that there was
anything doggedly dour about this one. Lancashire had a modest
lead on the first innings. At lunch time on the third day, Wednesday,
August 6, they were leading by 160 and had 5 second innings wickets
still intact. Major Booth, walking beside his captain, Sir Archie
White, as the Yorkshire team took the field, glanced back at the
clock on the pavilion tower. Afterwards he told historian 'Old
Ebor' that he had said: 'I think we can get them out in about an
hour and we shall then just have time to win.'

Booth then proceeded to demonstrate the practicability of his
assertion, taking 4 of the 5 wickets Lancashire lost for only 65 runs—
his final analysis on a fast batsman's wicket was 7 for 77. Rhodes and
Roy Kilner were soon out but Haigh and Benny Wilson, by forcing
batsmanship of the highest calibre, paved the way to victory with
108 runs in 50 minutes. With 71 runs still required and only 45
minutes left for play, excitement was feverish. So much so that the
spectators joined in, vying with each other to get the ball back to the
bowler with the minimum delay whenever a boundary was hit. Left-
hander Drake was kept back to avoid the time-consuming process of
field changing, but he went in when 26 runs were still needed—in 18
minutes. This target was reached and a handsome share in a great
victory was contributed by the skipper. Sir Archie was not out 27 and
the last of these invaluable runs had ensured a tie. An off drive for
four by Drake won the match with 6 minutes to spare and the crowd
surged round the pavilion demanded the appearance of the captain
to be personally and vociferously congratulated. They also called for
Hornby, the Lancashire captain, to show their appreciation of the
sporting spirit in which the game had been played throughout—no
bowling just to keep down the runs, no playing for a draw, just a flat
out bid for victory by both sides. The best Roses match ever? It

could be. At any rate Yorkshire sentiments at the time were summed
up in the remark of one Headingley customer well satisfied: 'Who
wouldn't pay a tanner to see a finish like this? Why, it's worth half a
dollar.'

7 Perfect Partnership

In another tremendous battle of Leeds, Yorkshire went down to Northamptonshire after a bonny fight—by twenty runs. Roy Kilner, aged twenty and in his second year with the county, gave rather more than a glimpse of the greatness that was to develop, very nearly making victory possible with an innings of true Yorkshire tenacity. When he was 91 and there were 4 wickets left with 33 runs to get, it seemed that the 'impossible' was to be achieved. But a pull fell short and, without Kilner at one end, the tail failed to stay. A welcome returning wanderer in August was E. Rockley Wilson, who had played for Yorkshire in 1899 when at Cambridge University, but had gone south and become a master at Winchester. He marked his return to the fold with a century against Essex at Bradford and his name appeared in second place in the averages.

For the first time since 1903, Hirst, out of the game too long through injury, failed to achieve the double. Rhodes was the only Yorkshire player to do so, but four of his colleagues, Hirst, Denton, Roy Kilner and B. B. Wilson all exceeded 1,000 runs, and Drake and Booth, in their last full season, 100 wickets. For both a great future seemed assured, with Test match honours regarded as a virtual certainty. As bowlers they had some outstanding joint successes, notably against Gloucestershire and Somerset. In both matches they bowled unchanged throughout.

Booth took 6 wickets and Drake 4 in each of Gloucester's innings and, in the Somerset game, Drake achieved the greatest feat in his short career—the bowler's dream of 'all ten'. In the first innings equality was maintained, Drake taking 5 wickets for 16, Booth 5 for 27. In the second, Drake took his 10 wickets for 35 runs in 8·5 overs of which 6 were maidens. It was said that Booth unselfishly tried to ensure that he would not rob Drake of his chance, bowling rather to keep the batsmen quiet than to get their wickets once the chance seemed to be within his grasp. Drake finished the season with 158 wickets, Booth with 155.

Alonzo Drake, from Honley, Huddersfield, was a droll fellow, full of good humour. When Jack Hobbs, in the course of a century of scintillating brilliance, hit off him a six—one of five in that unforgettable innings—smack into the face of the Bradford pavilion clock, pushing the hands back, he said to him: 'Nay, Jack, tha' should've knocked 'er on to 'arf past six and we'd 'a been rid of thee.' As the war drew inexorably nearer it was decided to let the Championship run its full course. The Scarborough Festival was, understandably, cancelled. And as 'the lights were going out all over Europe' to recall the Foreign Secretary's memorable words, reservists and Territorials disappeared, to be replaced by veterans and colts.

At Brighton, before the last pre-war game against Sussex started, Major Booth and Roy Kilner agreed to join up as soon as they returned home. With Dolphin they joined what was known as the 'Leeds Pals'. Booth, tall, dark, a 'character' and a cricketer of abundant promise, was killed, as was many another young second lieutenant, on that fateful day, July 1, 1916. Drake could not join the 'Pals'. He was rejected as medically unfit and, in fact, his health was such that he died soon after the war ended, at the age of 35. The loyalty of Yorkshire people to their county cricket club was vividly exemplified in the response to an appeal that they should continue to support it financially. Subscriptions rolled in, £5,560 worth of them, so that it was possible to keep the machine ticking over and to make donations to clubs, allowing them to keep grounds in some sort of order. Charity matches were organised. These continued at Leeds and other venues throughout the war and raised nearly £20,000. In addition, 500 pounds of cricket gear was sent to military camps at home and overseas. The Yorkshire C.C.C. offices became H.Q. of the West Riding Volunteers. Major Lord Hawke was County Adjutant and the County Club's Secretary, F. C. Toone, was Honorary Secretary. Three veterans of the pre-war Yorkshire sides, Rhodes, Hirst and Haigh, all went to work in a munitions factory at Huddersfield.

Yorkshire regarded with sadness and not a little apprehension their depleted ranks when the players assembled at Headingley to prepare for the first post-war cricket season, to be welcomed with joyful relief by those who had survived the horrors of trench warfare. They had relied, for bowling, almost entirely upon Drake and Booth, both now gone, and Rhodes, who was surely now a batsman rather than a bowler. But, as has happened so often when Yorkshire missed old stalwarts, new stars rose to shine, right from the start, or re-start.

One of them was a tousle-haired, determined bowler with a bounding run and considerable accuracy, Abram Waddington, who played for the Laisterdyke cricket club in his home town of Leeds and had had one trial in the Yorkshire 2nd XI just before the war. In his first match he took 4 Derbyshire wickets for 26 runs and, though this was at the beginning of July, he just reached 100 wickets by the season's end. He was ably supported by Rhodes, who proved that he was not just a batsman but could bowl as well as ever, by taking 142 wickets at 12·5 runs apiece. Emmott Robinson, though 'ancient' to play for his county for the first time—he was in his 36th year—had some good bowling performances, especially when he pitched 'em up wi't new ball and, above all, infused new life into the fielding by his example.

He was fearless and would crouch over the bat at very silly mid-on. Indeed, a batsman once suggested to him that the position was highly dangerous. Emmott's reply was typical. 'Never mind me, get on with thy lakin'.' The batsman was soon to pay for his impudence—'ct. Robinson'. In addition to these factors, Yorkshire had found a new and most excellent skipper in D. C. F. Burton, who had played under Sir Archie White before the war, a sound bat and often brilliant field at cover-point. But, without a doubt, the most significant aspect of the new Yorkshire was the coming together of Percy Holmes and Herbert Sutcliffe as opening batsmen.

Sutcliffe, like Waddington, made his impact on the team in July, when he was promoted from number seven to go in first with his older team mate. Whether or not it contributed to the perfect understanding which developed between them, the fact (affinity researchers please note) is that they shared a birthday, November 25. Holmes was the older by exactly seven years and had pre-war county experience, which gave him the confidence he was able to communicate to the lad fra' Pudsey. At any rate, over the Bank Holiday weekend, and against Lancashire, too, the pair earned lasting fame as a pair, with 253 superbly executed runs for the first wicket. Their debut as openers, in the Kent match at Headingley starting on June 30, had not been a resounding success.

Holmes was out for nought, but Sutcliffe demonstrated his class with 20 runs out of 64 fought for with rare skill on a nasty wicket relished by bowlers Woolley and Fairservice. Before the end of the season, however, the pair already had five century opening partnerships behind them (the final tally proved to be 74) including 279

Left: George Hirst coaching at Eton after a long and glorious career with Yorkshire—in 1906 he scored 2,385 runs and took 208 wickets, a unique feat. *Below:* The great Wilfred Rhodes, t' Pride o' Yorkshire, who, between 1898 and 1930 scored 39,797 runs and took 4,187 wickets.

Left: Yorkshire's famous opening partnership, Sutcliffe and Holmes, who still hold the first wicket record of 555, scored v. Essex in 1932.

Right: Don Bradman, then 21, acknowledges applause in his halcyon summer of 1930, the year he scored 334 (300 in one day) in the Test at Headingley.

against Northamptonshire—and five centuries each. Sutcliffe made manifest a big occasion temperament as well as power and a sure eye, by completing his hundred in that huge stand with a huge six. With such abundant new talent plus Rhodes, Hirst, Denton, Roy Kilner (recovered from a war wound) of the trusty old guard, it was no great surprise to the discerning that Yorkshire added another Championship to their lengthening list.

There was a wistful significance about Sutcliffe's highest score, 174, in that lustrous first season. It was scored at Dover, which he had last contemplated from a stretcher bringing him home from the war—dubious, indeed, about his cricketing future. Emmott Robinson, emerging as a character as well as a menacing new ball bowler, gave Yorkshire a promising start to the 1920 season, taking 9 Lancashire wickets for 36 runs to win a typically tense and swinging Roses encounter very much against the odds before his inspired assault. Lancashire's eminent opening pair, Makepeace and Hallows, had, overnight, hit 44 of the 188 runs required to win.

The first wicket fell to Robinson at 56 and four were down for 70. But Sharp and James Tyldesley then took their side to within 52 runs of victory which, with 6 wickets still standing, looked tolerably certain. Emmott Robinson, however, bowled with such venom and accuracy that all six fell to him for 29 runs, leaving Yorkshire unexpected victors by 22 runs. Robinson, acknowledging the gift to him by Mr Burton of the ball 'suitably inscribed', said that it was his inswinger that did for Lancashire. Certainly he bowled a near-unplayable ball, fast medium, on a perfect length, which pitched on the leg stump, streaked past the bat, and sent the off bail flying past first slip.

He had a highly individual run-up, with his own special hop in the middle of it. With flannels concertina-ed over his boots and toes turned in, no-one who had ever seen him before could possibly mistake him. Emmott was all Yorkshire, dedicated, fanatical. Cricket was his religion and cricket was Yorkshire cricket. When, in a Middlesex match, he dropped Hearne, he kept his head bowed low until at last he bowled him. And, when Yorkshire dismissed Derbyshire for 86, he moaned: 'They should never a' got them' repeating the phrase as he harked back for months to the lost opportunities of that day. At a crucial stage in a Roses match, after he had batted doggedly for a couple of hours, Abe Waddington jumped out to a ball and was stumped.

Such reckless folly positively preyed on Emmott's mind. 'Think of it, gettin' stoomped wi' t'match in that state—I'd a' died first' he mourned over and over again—it was said, for years rather than months. A wasted Yorkshire wicket, like a catch dropped by a Yorkshireman, was a catastrophe. Opposing batsmen were deadly foes to be despatched with the minimum of delay. Roy Kilner, whose Yorkshire fervour was enlivened by a rich humour, said of him that if he had taken 'all ten', he would have begrudged the chap who was not out. He never did, though his five entries under 'Exceptional Bits of Bowling' include two eights—for 32 against Northamptonshire and for 13 against Cambridge University.

In the season which brought him so near the longed-for 'all ten' he was less successful than Waddington and Rhodes, who had to bear the main bowling brunt, and shared between them 296 wickets, the other six bowlers used aggregating the remaining 181 between them. One side to give all of them 'the stick' was Hampshire, in a match which was the saddest memory for Yorkshire people since the Somerset tidal wave in 1901. On a beautifully sunny June Saturday, with the well-filled Headingley ground looking its verdant best, Brown and Bowell started the annihilation of the champions with an opening stand of 183.

At the close of play Brown, one of cricket's most versatile players, was 232 not out, and Philip Mead was on 122. The Hampshire total was 456 for 2. Both wickets had fallen to a fast bowler named Whiting, from Driffield, who had played in 1914 but was quickly to vanish from the first-class scene. The figures of the other Yorkshire bowlers were a sorry sight—Kilner 0 for 103, Waddington 0 for 96, Rhodes 0 for 69, Robinson 0 for 59. Then came rain, and, on Monday, the return of flaming June. On a 'sticky dog', Yorkshire could only muster 159 and 228, Hampshire coasting home by an innings and 72 runs. For Yorkshire there was one crumb of comfort —the imperturbably exemplary wicket-keeping of Dolphin, who conceded only two byes in that formidable Hampshire total.

However, revenge was sweet indeed when Yorkshire, in the return match, beat the impudent southerners on their own ground by an even bigger margin, an innings and 235. They had the immense satisfaction of seeing, upon the Portsmouth score board, these figures: total, 585; wickets down, 3; batsman number one, 302. This was the highest individual score of the season and a career record for Percy Holmes. Rhodes also had a great match, 63 not out and 11 wickets for 129 runs. Holmes had a wonderful season, hitting six more centuries and aggregating 2,144 runs with an average of 59 and not a duck against his name.

Holmes was dominant again in 1921, a year to be remembered with awe for the mighty deeds of mighty Armstrong's Australians and for a summer of rare sunshine. The latter aspect was not manifest during the Roses match at Headingley when, once more, rain robbed Yorkshire of the victory the August Bank Holiday weekend crowds had every right to expect. After dismissing Lancashire for 153, Yorkshire hit up 489, to which Holmes (following 52 not out in the previous Lancashire game) contributed 132. Lancashire still needed 192 to stave off an innings defeat when rain ended the match.

One great cricketer, John Berry Hobbs (I will not quarrel with Wilfred Rhodes' assessment that he was the greatest of all England batsmen) had vivid, if mixed memories of Headingley in 1921—memories of triumph and tribulation. Surrey played there in June and, as it eventuated, that was for Hobbs his only county match that summer. He had suffered a strain in May and was playing for the first time. That the enforced lay-off had not impaired his form was evident when, in his side's second innings he scored 172 not out towards a winning total of 294. Only a few days after this demonstration of Mastership, Hobbs was on the Headingley ground again for the third Test against the Australians.

After fielding all day he was taken ill in the evening and rushed to hospital, where his appendix was removed. England, one short and that one the most likely in a dubious assortment to influence the game in England's favour, faltered and tottered to defeat. Armstrong had brought with him not only Macartney, McDonald and Gregory but gremlins galore (or whatever were the equivalent creatures in those days). In the early stages of this ill-starred Test, J. W. H. T. Douglas had to leave the field owing to a bereavement, and Lionel Tennyson, promoted to acting captain, split a hand severely stopping a powerful drive.

The Headingley spectators were already morosely resentful at the dropping of Rhodes—inexplicably as they, and many of his loyal supporters outside the Ridings firmly believed. Had he not, on that very ground, when England were floundering to defeat in the second Test, hit an undefeated 267 and then taken 7 Leicestershire wickets for 66 runs? The Headingley congregation, with no local gods to worship, bestowed some affectionate attention upon the only

Yorkshire-born player taking part in the proceedings, Sammy Carter, the Australian wicket-keeper. He could be sure of hearty applause for every purposeful move, such as taking a fast one on the leg side and, indeed, virtually every sign of activity. There were, to be sure, at least two gems in that somewhat drab setting. One was a century of sheer beauty from the 'Governor General'.

The other was Lionel Tennyson's heroic and virtually one-handed defiance of Australia's ferociously fast bowlers, without which splendid siege Armstrong's men would have won by an even more contemptuous margin. Tennyson, his injured right hand heavily bandaged and used largely to keep the bat straight, an agonising process every ball he played, used his left hand with such adroitness and power that he scored 63 and 36 in England's innings of 259 and 202. The non-Debrett crowd rose to this Debrett 'foreigner' with the courage and belligerency of one of their own champion fighting cocks.

In Yorkshire circles, Rockley Wilson blossomed as a bowler of such relentless accuracy that he took 51 wickets during August, for only 11 runs each. Oldroyd, who had been a colt before the war, also came to flower as a dependable batsman (he actually scored more than 16,000 runs in the next decade though he was in his thirties at the start of it) and, at last, prayers for a quick bowler were answered, in the lean, wiry, grimly determined form of George Macaulay. He was not fast in the tradition of the great fast bowlers, rather medium-fast, with genuine finger spin and swing. On a 'sticky dog' his off-break could be unplayable.

His run was short, rather high-stepping, his action beautifully rhythmical. Both he and Waddington took more than 100 wickets. Rhodes again accomplished the double and five other batsmen also exceeded 1,000 runs—Holmes, Sutcliffe, Oldroyd, Robinson and Roy Kilner. Strong as they were, Yorkshire finished only fourth—due almost entirely to rain robberies in the early part of the season. This was hard luck on Mr Burton, a fine captain and useful performer, for the next year, under the captaincy of Geoffrey Wilson, with better weather luck, the team regained the Championship, which was to be theirs so often in the inter-war years. Still, Burton had led his team to the top in his first year as captain, as had Sir Archie White, though he was suffering from appendicitis when they clinched the matter. One of the season's outstanding feats was performed by Abe Waddington, who, at Hull, took 4 Sussex wickets before a run was scored and finished his 7 overs, 4 of them maidens, with 7 wickets for 6 runs. Sussex plummeted to their lowest ever total, 20, and lost by an innings though Yorkshire only scored 125, Arthur Gilligan the Sussex (and later, England) captain and fast bowler, taking 6 wickets for 20 runs. Once more the Hampshire matches provided surprise away wins for both sides. Yorkshire at home were out for 56 (Kennedy 7 for 28), Hampshire at home for 44 (Kilner 6 for 13).

For the first time, four Yorkshire bowlers, Rhodes, Kilner, Macaulay and Waddington, exceeded 100 wickets, and Yorkshire demonstrated their lofty superiority by winning ten matches by an innings. But the next season's record was even more remarkable. The Champions lost only one match out of 35—by 3 runs. That dramatic defeat was experienced at Headingley at the beginning of June in what was, for Yorkshire at such a peak, a low-scoring game. Nottinghamshire hit up 200, led on the first innings by 66, and then were all out for 95. Yorkshire's second innings started with a singular piece of ill-luck. Holmes, avoiding an express delivery from Matthews which kicked chest high on the leg side, touched his wicket, dislodging a bail. Nobody noticed it except John Gunn, who appealed from point. Holmes was given out, and did not dispute the decision, but the spectators roared their disapproval (whether or not they really knew what had happened) and much argument was heard thereafter. Still, it looked all Kirkstall Lane to a Trent Bridge lollipop on a Yorkshire win, especially when Rhodes and Kilner, the latter's cap characteristically askew and signalling confidence, had hit 56 runs in half an hour and only 36 more were needed with 5 wickets to fall. It was Staples who dramatically turned the tide.

8 Tall Scores

Powerful batting—a dozen times scores of over 300 were made—varied, accurate bowling, and exemplary fielding made Yorkshire (allowing for the one lapse) invincible. Ten counties were beaten twice, thirteen matches won by an innings (and, had there been time, the champions might well have made this figure fourteen, the prospective victims being a formidable Rest of England XI). Yorkshire, in 1924, became champions for the thirteenth time and Headingley was the scene of two unforgettable encounters; in one Yorkshire went down inexplicably and totally unexpectedly to (oh, dear!) Lancashire, and in the other, England casually disposed of a strong South African side—more formidable, perhaps, on their home matting wickets than on Yorkshire grass.

The first of these two memorable games was played in dreary weather over the Whitsun weekend. The match, in its early stages, was entirely in tune with the conditions, for Lancashire depressed the holiday crowd with a painful batting exhibition, taking four hours over a total of 113. Yorkshire took a slender but quietly encouraging lead, thanks to Kilner and Oldroyd; and Kilner, with Macaulay, proceeded to demolish the Lancastrians so that their faces were as red as their roses when they found themselves all back in the dressing rooms with a mere 74 on the board.

Kilner's analysis read 4 wickets for 13 runs and Macaulay's 4 for 19. All that mighty Yorkshire needed to win was a paltry 57. It was, it must be, a pushover. Few spectators were on the ground for what looked like a formality on the third day. Their anguish was awful to behold. In just 65 minutes Yorkshire-deported Cecil Parkin and Richard Tyldesley had made the very most of the teacherous pitch to spin out Yorkshire for 33. Tyldesley took 6 wickets for 18 runs, Parkin 3 for 15. Only Kilner, cap as defiant as ever, once again demonstrated Yorkshire doggedness. He was the only batsman to reach double figures and, in the lamentable circumstances, his 13 not out was a valiant effort. This painful episode has tended to eclipse the splendid deeds of that champion Yorkshire side—including four victories by an innings and ten by ten wickets. Sutcliffe scored 255 not out against Essex and 213 against Somerset. He, Holmes, Oldroyd, Leyland and Rhodes all totalled more than 1,000 runs.

As for the Headingley Test, it was such a comfortable win for England that it does not rank among the more exciting of international occasions. Hendren took a century off the South African bowling, Tate took nine of their wickets and Hobbs and Sutcliffe once more put on more than a hundred for England's first wicket.

The following year was shared, as to honour and glory, by Wilfred Rhodes, in his fiftieth year, and Roy Kilner, fifteen years his junior but with, as it so unhappily turned out, so little time to live. Both accomplished the double, Rhodes for the sixteenth time, and shared some winning partnerships, notably in the Derby fixture at Headingley when they scored more than 250 runs between them and took a major share of the wickets. The season opened in a somewhat speculative atmosphere. Yorkshire had not been the most popular of counties the previous year and there were unpleasant moments at Bramall Lane which led to reports by the umpires to the M.C.C. Their view was that the ugly barracking of the crowd had been invited by Abe Waddington's 'attitude towards decisions'. At any rate, Middlesex, Yorkshire's opponents in this less than happy game, threatened not to renew the fixture. This cloud, fortunately, dissolved and there is no doubt that the geniality of those great cricketers and joyous characters, Leyland and Kilner, had a considerable influence on the betterment of relations.

So, indeed, had firm captaincy by Major A. W. Lupton, who had succeeded Geoffrey Wilson. His personal performances, at the age of 46, would scarcely have justified his inclusion in the team. But that was the age of amateur captaincy and, to be sure, his leadership of a truly powerful team was entirely adequate as was suggested by its position at the head of the table with more than a 10 per cent lead over Surrey. The Headingley highlight was the benefit match for the vastly popular Roy Kilner, and Middlesex, all rancour gone, were his choice of opponents. There was no shortage of incidents, however, starting with the worrying absence of Percy Holmes. Leyland opened the Yorkshire innings with Sutcliffe and 218 runs were on the board before Leyland, at 110, gave a catch to Greville Stevens off express bowler Gubby Allen.

After the departure of Oldroyd, Holmes, who explained that he had been the victim of a rail delay, joined Sutcliffe in another century stand, and a dazzling one—135 runs in 100 minutes. Sutcliffe reached 235 and Yorkshire 528 for 6, at which score Lupton declared. Kilner, to the bitter disappointment of the hero-worshippers all round the ground, was run out with his score 15. He took one wicket in each Middlesex innings, the match petering out in a draw. However, it was a resounding success financially. The attendance totalled 71,000 (unbelievable today!) and Roy's benefit fund reached a record, up to then, £4,016 19s. to be exact.

The Australians were here again in 1926, imperishable in the memory for the General Strike, which paralysed the country and made transport to cricket for the early games a walking matter. This unprecedented upheaval having subsided, the hitherto triumphant Australians, though a side equipped for much run-getting, had to concede that, if the scoring could be heavy the rain could be heavier. After four drawn Tests England gloriously recovered the Ashes at the Oval, Hobbs and Sutcliffe embellishing the records with a magnificent second innings opening stand, Sutcliffe finishing with 161 and Hobbs 100 (about which division of spoils Wilfred Rhodes had something to say, as I have already recorded). But the Test match standing out as one of the most eventful of all the draws in the long series of England-Australia contests, took place at Headingley. The first sensational occurrence was the decision of England, and Nottinghamshire, captain A. W. Carr, having won the toss from H. L. ('Horseshoe') Collins, to put Australia in first. The wicket was soft but certainly not difficult. The ground had been virtually waterlogged the evening before and there had been some morning sun. Carr (mistakenly as things turned out) evidently gambled on this climatic sequence producing a pitch imbued with some devil.

However, it was not Carr's day. He had seemed more than justified when Sutcliffe caught Warren Bardsley off Tate's, and the game's, first ball. The fifth ball of that same over Macartney edged to Carr at slip—and he dropped it. What the effect on Australian morale of a first over score reading 2 for 2 (whether you put the runs first, as we do, or the wickets, as they do) we can only ponder. Macartney quite cheerfully, as well as majestically, took advantage of this lapse, scoring a century before lunch—a feat he twice accomplished there— and proceeding to 151. Woodfull, 'the unbowlable', hit 141 exemplary runs, and A. J. Richardson 100, in a total of 494. England, in spite of a face-saving, tail-end century stand by bowlers Macaulay and

Geary, had to follow on, Hobbs (88) and Sutcliffe (94) imperturbably building up a second innings aggregate of 254 for 3. This partnership, and the ever returning rain, turned the game once more and ensured the draw, which was not, all changes of fortune considered, an unreasonable result.

It was, indeed, a superb recovery, Hobbs and Sutcliffe put on 156 invaluable runs before Hobbs brought his quite faultless innings to an end playing a ball from Grimmett on to his stumps. In the process he set up a new test match aggregate record, beating Clem Hill's 2,660, a feat not unappreciated by the gathering; nor was Percy Chapman's glorious 40 out of 42 runs in a quarter of an hour.

Carr did not escape post mortem criticism. *Wisden* in its review of the Tests, recorded that at Leeds, 'an unfortunate course of action, in giving Australia first innings, courted disaster, England's batsmen extracting themselves from a dangerous situation in most convincing fashion.'

The Headingley faithful could not complain about lack of entertainment upon their own ground in the 1927 County Championship matches. The wicket, much less soporific than it had often been, proved very friendly to the bowlers on more than one occasion, obligingly providing both turn and kick.

Worcestershire were victims of this impishness. Robinson and Macaulay bowled unchanged through both their innings of 48 and 81, the former's match record being 8 for 65 and that of the latter 12 for 50. For Macaulay it was an unforgettable game. When Fred Root had reduced Yorkshire to a paltry 94 for 7, Macaulay and fellow bowler Waddington set about the bowling with determination and power, scoring 163 runs in 85 minutes. Waddington achieved his only century in first class cricket, 111, and the spectators regarded themselves as more than adequately rewarded. The cunning left-arm combination of Kilner and Rhodes disposed of Surrey, one of the most formidable of batting sides, for 172 and 203, Kilner returning 4 for 39 and 5 for 76, Rhodes 5 for 59 and 2 for 69.

Surrey were not at all happy about this state of affairs and there was much grumbling about the wicket which (said the Surrey men), had been treated with too much sand. This argument was unconvincing in the light of Herbert Sutcliffe's treatment of the Surrey bowling. He batted rather more than four hours in the soundest fashion, to reach 176 out of 333. Leyland scored 70 and Oldroyd 52 not out, but the gap between these three and the next batsman's 8 suggested that something more earthly than pixies *had* affected the pitch.

The Lancashire match proved to be a mighty duel between Herbert Sutcliffe and Ernest Tyldesley. In the first innings Sutcliffe demonstrated his entire worthiness to open the England batting with Hobbs, mastering the bowling which so baffled his colleagues, to score 95 invaluable runs in a meagre total of 157. The second highest scorer also justified his earlier appearances with Hobbs as England's batting spearhead, though he was content just to stay there, collecting a modest 18 in the process. Rhodes was the stout defender's name and as he took 3 Lancashire wickets including that of Tyldesley, who hit 165, he could be said to have contributed, as on so many occasions, to Yorkshire's avoidance of defeat. Sutcliffe's second innings score, 135, made very sure of denying a red rose triumph though Lancashire had led by 200 in the first innings.

There was poignancy, though none could possibly have sensed it, about the end of season fixture at Hove, distinguished by the all-round proficiency of Roy Kilner. He registered his highest score of the season, 91 not out, ensuring a useful lead over Sussex, and then took 3 wickets for 45 runs followed by 5 for 21 to win the game—his last for Yorkshire. As he had in previous winters, Kilner went to India to play and coach, at the invitation of the Maharajah of Patiala. In a minor match he scored 283, which was his last big innings. He contracted enteric fever, returned home a very sick man, and died in the Kendray Fever Hospital, Barnsley, aged 37, just before the new season was about to start.

Not far short of 150,000 lined the streets of his native Wombwell for his funeral. Today there is a street named after him, and the number of grizzled Tykes named Roy in his honour is still considerable. He is remembered, perhaps, with more affection than any of his contemporaries. For Roy Kilner was irrepressible, sometimes to the despair of die-hard disciplinarian Emmott Robinson and, come to that, of Rhodes too. 'Will't never get any sense?' Emmott would enquire after a particularly happy-go-lucky 'dip'—Kilner could never resist for long the temptation to have a go on the offside, especially with the cover drive. His humour was wry but never wounding. Describing the tenseness of the Roses matches he said, thoughtfully: 'We'll say "Good morning", then never speak again for three days.' And on cricket in general: 'What is wanted is no umpires and fair cheating all round.'

Yorkshire now wore a different look. Dolphin had left after twenty-two years of splendid service behind the stumps; so had Waddington, who was not satisfied with the terms of re-engagement. And a successor had to be found to Major Lupton. There was much consternation among the traditionalists when it became known that Sutcliffe had been offered the captaincy. 'A professional captain? disastrous, sir'—'Why not, pray?'—'Unthinkable'—'Progressive'. Thus the arguments raged. There was no comment to be had from Lord Hawke, which was scarcely surprising in view of his earlier prayer, or from Yorkshire Secretary, F. C. Toone, who had had the task of cabling the offer to Sutcliffe, touring South Africa with the M.C.C. team under Lt. Col. R. T. Stanyforth. And it was Sutcliffe who ended the controversy by turning down the captaincy he would surely have coveted. The correspondence is worth recording. Mr Toone wrote to Sutcliffe:

'Dear Herbert,
At the committee meeting yesterday you were appointed Captain for 1928 without your status being altered.
It is hoped that this will be agreeable to you and that you will accept the same and be happy and successful in your new and honoured position.

Best Wishes,
Yours sincerely,
F. C. Toone, Secretary'

Sutcliffe's cable was sent to Lord Hawke. It read: 'Official invitation received yesterday. Many thanks you and committee great honour. Regret to decline. Willing to play under any captain elected.'

The captain elected, at a special meeting of the committee, was W. A. Worsley, now Sir William Worsley Bart., President of Yorkshire C.C.C. and father of the Duchess of Kent, the Club's Patroness.

One, two, three, four . . . Yorkshire seemed to be on the slide when this comparatively lowly position was all that crowned the efforts of that 1928 season. Indeed, without Kilner and Waddington, with Rhodes nearing his 50th birthday and Robinson his 45th, the bowling could not be what it once had been. Certainly Rhodes confounded those who dared to suggest that he was too old at 49 by taking 10 Leicester wickets at Headingley, and Robinson, virtually solo, dismissed Cambridge University for 30, taking 8 wickets for 13.

But the old penetration was sometimes lacking. Yorkshire's

batting, however, was powerful, with Sutcliffe in such tremendous form that he topped the much desired, and nowadays apparently unattainable 3,000 runs mark, had an all match average of over 76 and a championship average of 85·48. He and Holmes shared eleven more century first wicket partnerships including, to the delight of both of them and of a fervent Headingley crowd, 290 in Yorkshire's second innings on the occasion of Holmes' benefit match. Holmes was top scorer in the match with 179 not out after 53 in the first innings. This tremendous stand was hailed with uninhibited delight not only because of the popularity of Percy Holmes but because Yorkshire had followed on, Middlesex having scored 488, Hendren contributing 169 and F. T. Mann 122. In Yorkshire's first innings Robinson had hit 70 not out and Arthur Wood, who had succeeded Arthur Dolpin as stumper and was to prove himself a more than useful bat as well as a true Yorkshire character of much humour and boundless dedication, a valuable 62.

These two figured in another splendid stand in the Roses game when Yorkshire were struggling to reach Lancashire's 385, after Holmes and Sutcliffe had opened with a superb run-a-minute 142. Yorkshire eventually led by 88—and then time ran out, the Lancashire innings having occupied seven and a half hours.

9 The Don Flows On

The Leeds Test of 1929, England v South Africa, was illuminated by a gay century from the flailing bat of H. G. Owen-Smith, widely known as 'Tuppy', Oxford triple blue, his other sports being rugby and boxing. He drove with power, displaying a special predilection for slow bowling, which he also pulled purposefully with the help of an exceptionally good eye. He hit two 6s and fifteen 4s. A last wicket stand by 'Tuppy' and A. J. Bell, South Africa's opening bowler, took the score from 172 to 275—103 in 65 minutes, setting up a new South African record. The Headingley crowd cheered as if both had been born within sound of the bells of St Michael's. This sparkling partnership tended to overshadow two quite superlative batting performances by Frank Woolley, bringing him 83 and 95 not out, and (with his own 3 wickets for 35 runs) ensuring, after many anxious moments, victory for England by 5 wickets. Rhodes, within three months of his fifty-second birthday, was the hero of the Sussex match at Leeds, saving a sagging side with scores of 43 and 55 and 3 valuable wickets. His was a noble role, too, in the Surrey match on the same ground, chosen by Sutcliffe for his richly deserved benefit—5 good wickets for only 34 runs.

Sutcliffe most certainly deserved a better fate than that which was his—a Saturday so wet that not a ball was bowled. The receipts were heavily affected but the benefit fund topped £3,000, the highest since Kilner's. Sutcliffe himself, with his old partner, Holmes, put on 77 runs in 80 minutes, which gave much pleasure to his hosts of admirers. Sutcliffe's score was 43, just one run fewer than that of his international partner, Hobbs, upon the other side. The match, much in Yorkshire's favour, was drawn.

The rather dismal season, weather-wise, which followed in 1930, was notable in cricket history generally and the Headingley annals particularly, for the spectacular success of twenty-one-year-old Donald George Bradman. In the third Test match at Headingley, the Australian captain, Woodfull, having won the toss and elected to bat, Bradman scored a century before lunch—102 out of 127 runs in just 95 minutes—and proceeded to add two more to it that day. Out of an Australian total of 566, Bradman, in six hours and a quarter, hit 334 (309 on the first day, the rest in 20 minutes on the second), which mammoth score included forty-six 4s and six 3s. Many of these came from powerful driving but there were some scintillating cuts and leg shots behind the wicket as well, to show the astonished spectators that he could be an artist as well as a batting machine of immense precision and power.

Don (later, as a mark of deep respect, The Don) was dubbed the Lindrum of cricket which indicated, simply, that he was in a class by himself, as then was his compatriot, Walter Lindrum, in the realm of billiards. And *Wisden* was moved to say of the Leeds Test that it 'afforded that remarkable young batsman, Bradman, the opportunity of leaving all individual batting records in representative matches far behind'. In the course of this relentless and chanceless innings young Bradman beat the 27-year-old record—287—set up by R. E. Foster at Sydney, and exceeded 1,000 runs in Test cricket. To say that he dominated this Leeds Test is no overstatement. The next highest Australian scores were 77 by Kippax and 50 by Woodfull. And Bradman, as if challenging the status of the greatest of all our batsmen, ran out Hobbs, with his score 13, by means of a brilliant throw-in from deep mid-off. In the testing circumstances of such tremendous scoring Maurice Tate did well indeed to take 5 wickets for 124 runs in 39 overs. Richard Tyldesley had 2 wickets for 104 and Harold Larwood 1 for 139—such was Bradman's attitude to the fastest bowler of his time.

England's reply of 391 was not negligible—in spite of Grimmett's guile, which brought him 5 wickets. Hammond got 113, firmly and exquisitely, Chapman 45 and Leyland 44. Hammond also scored 35, out of 95 for 2, in England's second innings and the game, which had been characterised by a truly remarkable triple century, a fierce thunderstorm, and some atrociously bad light, fizzled out in a draw. England's fielding, not for the first or the last time at Headingley, compared unfavourably with that of Australia and, come to that, with their previous performances. Bradman must be ranked the batsman of that year, with more than 2,000 runs and an average of 99·08 but, had it not been an Australian tour year, Maurice Leyland might well have achieved this unofficial title. Certainly he towered above them all in the Roses match at Leeds, hitting 211 not out, the highest score in that dour, twice yearly clash, following a fine innings memorable for confident and elegant shots all round the wicket, with 4 Lancashire victims for 49 runs. The measure of Leyland's dominance may be gauged by the other scores in Yorkshire's 417 for 9 wickets. Oldroyd was second highest scorer with 49, followed by Robinson, 41 and Sutcliffe, 40. Leyland followed this feat with 172 and 186 in the Middlesex and Derbyshire games.

If there had been a popularity poll, the candidates being cricketers playing between the wars, Maurice Leyland would have stood a very good chance of winning it. Cheerful, burly, as Yorkshire as 'Ilkla' Moor'—which folk ballad he would whistle just as thoughtfully in moments of triumph as in those of crisis, when he was so often called upon for rescue and so rarely failed to perform it. Leyland was one of many outstanding characters in the Yorkshire and Headingley story. Yet he had a special place, a niche all to himself. For more than a quarter of a century he exemplified all that was best in Yorkshire cricket. He was one of the most dependable of left-hand batsmen and, like many left-handers, had a graceful and flowing style. He could be and often was a forceful hitter; he was a rare fighter in a grim situation, a fine fielder and a versatile bowler with the 'chinaman' (like Compton later) up his sleeve for the likely victim. His cap angle was peculiarly his own, not to be compared with Roy Kilner's—a gentle tilt towards the right eye rather than a rakish leftward slope. His humour was dry but gentle. He was virtually never ruffled and his calm confidence, his bluff kindliness, helped many a young cricketer over a nervous, or even plain disastrous, start. Even Hutton.

When the greatest of Yorkshire batsmen, in his first match for his county, was run out for a duck, Leyland, with a friendly grin, commented: 'Never mind, lad, you're starting at the bottom.' Just four years later he stayed with Hutton half the time he was making the fabulous 364 at the Oval. The pair put on 382 runs and Leyland's share took $6\frac{1}{2}$ hours. In reply to criticism of this unusual sloth he replied cheerfully: 'Well, you see, I'm playing for my place.' Leyland's philosophy was crystallised in this immortal sentence: 'Well, there you are, out in t'middle and there's 30,000 people round t'boundary, and they can all play t'bowling better than you can. You've got to do summat.'

There was, in fact, a wry point about his quip on playing for his place. He had been dropped from the previous Test team. At the end

of Hutton's long, long innings everyone, naturally enough, wanted to
celebrate. Leyland led the way to the bar and ordered two bottles of
champagne. 'Why two bottles?' Len Hutton prudently enquired.
'One for thee, Len, and one for me' his partner for so long replied.
The dogged rescue work Leyland was so often called upon to perform,
and his humour, were both exemplified in the 1937 Test match against
Australia at Melbourne. England had followed on and still wanted
more than 300 runs with 5 wickets only left, to avert an innings
defeat. Leyland had been defending dourly when Walter Robins,
near the end of the day's play, joined him and promptly hit one
through the covers. As he galloped past for a quick third run Leyland
called out: 'What's your hurry, Mr Robins?—we shan't get 'em
tonight.' Leyland could, and often did, from sheer necessity, play
the straightest of straight bats with bowler-needling persistence. But
he could, and often did, hit out, not only with much aggression, but
with the grace characteristic of so many great left-handers. In
a long and illustrious career he hit 80 centuries, 9 for England
(including one in his first Test) scoring 33,600 runs. For Yorkshire
he hit nearly 27,000 runs, took 411 wickets and held innumerable
catches.

He headed the Yorkshire batting averages that peaceful summer
of 1930, when the world seemed a good place to live in and no-one
dreamed of taking Hitler seriously. The Lancashire match at
Headingley was a characteristically dour affair. Sutcliffe, quite unlike
himself, took two hours over 40 runs (his previous six scores against
the old enemy being 95, 135, 140, 126, 69 and 106). The result, with
rain a factor, was a tame draw. The new captain, for one year only as
scholastic duties were to claim him, was A. T. Barber and, under
him, Yorkshire remained third in the Championship. For Wilfred
Rhodes, in his 53rd year, this was the last season. Two bright
prospects headed the bowling averages, Verity and Bowes. But
Rhodes was third—and he was also in the top half of the batting
averages, a respectable enough finale.

He had outlived, in the playing sense, all his contemporaries. He
had bowled at every great batsman in the world from Grace and
Trumper to Bradman and Woolley. He had batted against the
world's best bowlers, from Kortright and Barnes to Larwood and
Grimmett. And he had himself excelled, year after year, in both
capacities. But with Verity to replace him in the attack, as he had
replaced Peel, the Yorkshire tradition was maintained. Woolley,

having hit young Hedley for six more than once in a big score, gruffly acknowledged: 'This chap bowls quite well.'

The year 1931 was one of true splendour for Yorkshire generally and Sutcliffe in particular. The former won the Championship, well before the end of the season, for the 15th time. Sutcliffe came near to a century average—in county games it was 97·57. His grand total of runs was 3,006 and he hit thirteen hundreds, nine of them for Yorkshire. The season's first match at Headingley resulted in an overwhelming victory for the county and early justification of Frank Woolley's guarded words. Warwickshire scored 201 and Yorkshire, given the familiar good send-off by Holmes and Sutcliffe (120) led by 97 just before tea on the second day. There was no play necessary on the third day!

Verity, overnight, had personally disposed of Warwickshire, taking all 10 wickets for 36 runs in 18·4 overs of which 6 were maidens. Yorkshire did not win again for a month when they found themselves eighth in the table. Thereafter 13 out of 15 matches were won, the other two drawn, and the Championship won by mid-August. Holmes and Sutcliffe piled on 309 runs in 220 minutes against poor old Warwick in the return fixture, and 323 in 4½ hours against Lancashire. Verity and Bowes again headed the bowling. But the greatest achievements of Holmes and Sutcliffe, the most prolific opening pair of their era, and of Verity, left hand bowler of relentless accuracy and much guile, were registered in the following season, when Yorkshire composedly retained the Championship.

The trio devastatingly dominated the Nottinghamshire match at Headingley, which provided one of the most astounding triumphs in the County's story. Notts batted first, scoring 234, in reply to which Yorkshire could only manage 163 for 9. Then a thunderstorm stopped play and it could not be resumed until the morning of the last day. Greenwood, who had succeeded Barber as captain, declared, relinquishing the slender chance of a first innings lead, and, by lunch, Notts were 38 for 0. Twenty-one runs later they were all out. Verity, for the second time in his short but glorious career, had taken all ten wickets, this time for only ten runs, scored in less than four overs—the other sixteen overs he bowled were maidens. He accomplished the hat-trick and twice had two wickets in succession. What had seemed an inevitable draw, with Notts deservedly taking first innings points, was suddenly, dramatically, an open game offering a distinct chance to Yorkshire. This was elegantly, chancelessly and speedily taken by Holmes and Sutcliffe, who hit the required 139 runs in 90 minutes.

Verity's considerable part in a colossal victory over Essex was, understandably, overshadowed by the astounding feat of Holmes and Sutcliffe. Just before one o'clock on the second day they had established a new world record first wicket partnership, 555, beating the record set up by their predecessors, Brown and Tunnicliffe, 34 years earlier. Holmes had given one chance, at 4, but otherwise played quite faultless cricket, though suffering acutely from lumbago. Both were, understandably, a trifle stiff upon the second day, having scored between them 423 runs on the first. The unlikely target having been reached, Sutcliffe, his own score 313, appeared to give himself up, Eastman bowling him. As he departed for the pavilion, leaving Holmes with a modest, uncompleted 224, the applause was thunderous but, it was obvious that the scorers had run into some snag. The scoreboard was wavering uncertainly, first proclaiming the total 555, then 554.

Had they broken the record? Or hadn't they? There was an hour of frantic recounting. While telegrams arrived in a steady stream scorebooks were checked and rechecked. At last, a no-ball solved the riddle. New record it was. Essex were subsequently dismissed for 78 and 164, Verity taking 5 wickets for 8 runs and 5 for 45, Bowes, 4 for 38 and 5 for 47. A wonderful season brought them 162 and 190 wickets respectively. A bowler of somewhat less renown, H. Fisher, assured himself a niche in the county's history with a hat-trick unique.

Against Somerset at Bramall Lane he hit upon the pads successively, and in the same spot, N. S. Mitchell-Innes, Andrews and Luckes, the wicket-keeper. At each appeal for l.b.w., the umpire's finger went up, the last time with a slowness suggestive of incredulity. And, as it rose, the umpire was heard to murmur: 'As Gawd is my witness.' The umpire was, indeed, that irrepressible character, Leicester's former fast bowler, Alec Skelding.

Sutcliffe exceeded even his tally of the year before, compiling 3,336 runs, including fourteen centuries. Leyland, Holmes, Mitchell and Barber all amassed more than 1,000 runs and Yorkshire reigned supreme. That shrewd judge from Lord's, Harry Lee, asserted that the 1933 Yorkshire side was the best he had ever seen and he would have liked to have been able to jump back in time and match them with the Middlesex team of 1921. Sellers had taken over from

Greenwood and, fine captain though he undoubtedly was, such was the team under his command that it was said that all he had to do was to win the toss. Bowes, Verity and Macaulay were the virtually irresistible attacking force—they shared 391 wickets between them in championship matches—Sutcliffe, Leyland and Mitchell the all-conquering run-getters, one of the most prolific trios in the history of the championship.

All three hit more than 2,000 runs that season and, adding generously to this prodigality was Barber, with well over 1,500. Yorkshire's record at Headingley that year was such that southern and midland folk retreated not merely licking their wounds, but filled with gloom and despondency. Once mighty Kent struggled to 90, followed on, achieved a slightly more encouraging 172—and still were beaten by an innings. Bill Bowes had a remarkable match, taking 6 wickets for 44 and 6 for 73. Warwickshire players felt quite perky when the supreme Yorkshiremen compiled only 229. Their reply deflated them completely, 63 and 101, Verity taking, in all, 9 wickets for 43 runs. In the Northamptonshire fixture, the visitors fared even worse and Verity better. They scored 63 and 135 (Verity 7 for 35 and 6 for 67) in reply to Yorkshire's 349 for 7, to which Leyland contributed 192 (a total he beat at Dover, scoring 210 not out after Verity had taken 9 Kent wickets for 59—yet Yorkshire lost!). To offset the steam-roller victories there were some setbacks, including the Dover shock. Sussex beat Yorkshire twice but, before the second of these matches, at Hove and, indeed, before the Kent game, Yorkshire were sure of the championship. Perhaps the most severe jolt came at Leeds, their happy hunting ground that year. Lancashire took a substantial lead to make sure of first innings points in the Roses battle.

10 Verity the Great

The Australians were here again in 1934 and this welcome visit was held by the devotees to be the only reason Yorkshire lost the Championship. Certainly Leyland and Verity played in all five Tests, Sutcliffe in four and Bowes in three. At Lord's Verity set up a new Test match record with 14 Australian wickets in one day. And this was, for Leyland, not only his benefit year but a year of personal triumph. He was, by far, England's most successful batsman, with 478 runs and an average of 68·28. Sutcliffe was second with 304 runs, average 50·66 (compared, to be fair, to the Aussies, with Ponsford's 94·83 and Bradman's 94·75). Verity and Bowes took 43 wickets between them, no mean share of the spoils. The Leeds Test, though drawn, remains indelible in the memory of all who were fortunate enough to be present, for Don Bradman's second triple century upon that ground. The first day's play went to the bowlers, which was inexplicable on a wicket described by Bob Wyatt as 'feather bed'. England were all out for 200 and only C. F. Walters (44) played with any real confidence. O'Reilly (3 for 46) and Grimmett (4 for 57) were the chief executioners. However, Australian wickets fell too, 3 of them for 39 runs by the close of play.

A low scoring match seemed likely—until Ponsford and Bradman got going. When stumps were drawn on the second day Ponsford was 181 and Bradman not out 271. Bradman had been merciless, machine-like in his infallibility. He had driven Bowes for two 4s off the first two balls of the day, as if firing a couple of warning shots across our bows. Thereafter nothing caused the master to falter or even seem to hurry a single shot. But the score proceeded to pile up at the rate of 70 runs to the hour. In the midst of this cascade, the Headingley crowd (by now Bradman fans anyway) was reduced to far deeper gloom by the news that Yorkshire, star-starved, had been beaten by Warwickshire.

It was dominant batting, rather than any lapses in the field, which took Australia's score to 584 on the third day. Wyatt's fielding, in particular, had been brilliant and the bowlers never relaxed their efforts. Bowes, after that daunting start, had the satisfaction of bowling Bradman when he had reached 304—and the appreciative spectators formed a human corridor all the way from the wicket slapping Bradman's damp back as no Aussie's back had been slapped before. Bowes finished with a highly creditable 6 wickets for 142 runs in 50 overs, of which 13 were maidens. Walters once more looked more like a Test batsman than some of his fellows when England batted again, and he was not out 45 when a storm flooded the ground and saved us from defeat.

Sir Neville Cardus (in his book, *Good Days*) was scathing about England's batting. 'They turned their bats into crutches of senility' he wrote. There was nothing crutch-like, however, about Leyland's bat in the series or the season. In the Tests he hit 109 at Lord's, 153 at Manchester, and 110 at the Oval. In his own benefit match at Headingley he did not sparkle to this extent, his contributions being 8 and 32 not out, plus 3 wickets for 35 in Nottinghamshire's second innings. But Yorkshire won by 9 wickets and the fund plus collection brought him £3,648 7s. 4d., the highest benefit apart from Kilner's, up to that time.

Sutcliffe, though still among the 'greats', was passing his fabulous peak—the last of the century partnerships with Holmes was now behind him. But as so often before, a new star was already rising to take his place. Young Len 'Ooten, fra' Poodsey, had his first trial in the county side. Sutcliffe himself had watched Hutton and, with remarkable prescience, had acclaimed him as potentially one of the greatest of all batsmen. His career started with that duck already recorded but, in his second match, against Oxford University, he was at the wicket three hours and, against Warwickshire, he hit 196, the third highest score of any Yorkshire player that season (beaten only by Barber, 248, and Sutcliffe himself, 203).

The Headingley spectators had the great gratification of witnessing most effective Yorkshire participation in the 1935 Test, which was against the South Africans, captained by H. F. Wade. Arthur Mitchell, playing in his first Test match and before his own folk, helped Wally Hammond to build up a modestly respectable total, despite the frailty of other batsmen. In England's first innings of 216 he scored 58 to Hammond's 63 and, in the second innings of 278 for 7 declared, 72 to Hammond's 87 not out. Bowes and Verity took two wickets each in South Africa's first innings total of 171 and Bowes two in the second, 194 for 5, rain and bad light having ensured a draw.

Smailes, a useful new ball bowler who could hit the ball too, had a big share in Yorkshire's victory over Sussex at Leeds, scoring 89—Barber was top scorer with 191—and taking 6 wickets in the match. But the bowling feat of the year belonged to Bill Bowes. After taking 6 Lancashire wickets for 16 to skittle the old enemy for a puny 53, against Northants he took 8 wickets for 18 and 8 for 17, oddly enough with almost precisely the same number of balls in each innings, 88 and 89.

The season of 1936 was a dismal one, wet and often cold. But it's an ill wind. Verity found consolation for the conditions in a harvest of 216 wickets. He and Bowes continued to bear the brunt of the attack, the third 'spearhead' bowler being Smailes, in place of Macaulay. These three all reached three figures and finished in this order in the bowling averages—Bowes, Verity, Smailes, followed, it is worth noting, by Hutton, whose 21 wickets were not expensive. The Surrey match at Headingley was notable—and significant—for a great stand between the veteran and the tyro, both immortals, Sutcliffe and Hutton, the former scoring 129, the latter 163. Yorkshire declared their innings closed at 519 for 6, to win by an innings and 185 runs. Sellers, never one to sit back and await events, took drastic action to ensure the taking of the new ball which was so much to the liking of Smailes. With Surrey's second innings score 186 he put himself on and gave away thirteen runs by the simple expedient of delivering four byes and nine wides. Smailes responded to this sacrifice by polishing off Surrey to return 4 for 21. Bowes' figures were 5 for 24 and 2 for 17.

The year following, politically overshadowed by the sinister activities of the ranting, snarling Adolf Hitler, building up a mighty war machine, yelling for 'lebensraum' and generally demonstrating that he was, as the old lady put it, 'a proper fidget', will be remembered, in the more pacific world of cricket, for a titanic championship struggle. Yorkshire won it, pressed all the way by Middlesex. As the issue was in doubt until the last fixtures, the added interest in the county programme was clearly more than an escape from all the horrid noises across the channel and the unheeded but chilling warnings frequently uttered by a far-seeing Englishman named Winston Churchill.

The New Zealanders, who were so soon to be fighting by our side,

were our touring opponents and young Hutton played in his first
Tests against them, scoring a hundred in the second. He also hit a
century off their far from negligible bowling for Yorkshire at
Headingley—135 out of the county's total of 364. The match was a
draw but the finish was extremely exciting. Martin Donnelly, a left
handed bat beautiful to watch and in the Woolley tradition, had hit
97 for New Zealand in their second innings. When the ninth wicket
fell 150 runs were still required so that a Yorkshire victory, with only
twenty minutes left, seemed assured. However, E. W. Tindall and J.
Cowie refused to budge. At the end of the twenty minutes each had
scored one run and defeat had been, with a dourness hitherto almost
a Yorkshire prerogative, averted.

Verity had a splendid match against Warwickshire, taking 9 for 43
and 5 for 49. Sutcliffe and Hutton hit exactly 75 each and Yorkshire
won by 9 wickets. In the latter part of the season, so keen was the
Yorkshire-Middlesex rivalry for the title that Walter Robins, the
Middlesex captain, sent a telegram to Yorkshire captain Brian
Sellers suggesting a four-day challenge match whatever the Championship result. This was played on neutral ground, the Oval, and
Yorkshire beat the runners-up by an innings. Hutton, that year, left
no doubt as to his status, scoring 8 centuries, including one in the
challenge game, and aggregating nearly 3,000 runs. Norman Yardley,
down from Cambridge University, was reported to have been
'hailed by good judges as a coming England batsman'.

11   Casualties—and a 'Character'

The 1938 Headingley Test against Bradman's Australians was sand-
wiched between the Old Trafford wash-out (literally—not a ball was
bowled) and the Oval run-glut in which Hutton took 13 hours and 20
minutes to set up the new individual record of 364. It is perhaps idle,
but also difficult to refrain from speculating what would have been
the outcome of the Leeds match had it not been for the Middlesex v
Yorkshire game which preceded it.

That match, played at Lord's, changed drastically the composition
of the England team. During it Hutton, Leyland and Gibb were all
injured and could not even be considered. Walter Robins had put
Yorkshire in on a wicket which turned out to be a flyer. The fast
bowlers, Smith, Gray and Edrich, with no more malice in their hearts
than the desire to take some Yorkshire wickets, were positively
dangerous. One ball broke Hutton's finger, another Leyland's thumb,
and a third hit Paul Gibb's head. All three were to play at Leeds—
Gibb, who had kept wicket with much success for Cambridge
University and for the Gentlemen, in place of Ames, temporarily out
of the game. Wood, of Yorkshire, was considered as a substitute, but
Price, of Middlesex, was preferred; a choice which met with some
criticism on the ground that it would lengthen an already long tail,
and that Wood, if less agile than once he was, had vast experience,
could hang on as a batsman, and was a Yorkshireman on his own
'mook 'eap', too.

At Headingley, Hammond won the toss and decided to bat. Barnett
opened with Edrich. The weather was gloomy, a dull day with mist
hanging over the ground and some moisture in the wicket. Barnett
was clearly below his splendid best and was twice dropped off Waite
in the first few overs. However, it was the more confident Edrich
who was to go first, bowled by one of O'Reilly's sizzling off-breaks.
Indeed, not for the first time or the last, O'Reilly proved to be the
most menacing and successful bowler on either side. Bradman, and,
to a lesser extent, Hammond dominated the batting.

Hammond was unusually subdued to start with, and the score was a meagre 62 at lunch time. Afterwards, however, he raised the scoring rate with some glorious shots, including a flashing four through the covers off McCormick, two off-driven fours off the conquering O'Reilly, and a gorgeous six high over mid-off. But, in the end, O'Reilly bowled him, his score 76. Barnett (Australia) who had caught Barnett (England), then stumped Paynter and, once a useful stand between bowlers Verity—who received a vociferous welcome—and Doug Wright had been broken, England were quickly all out for 223. The confidence of Australia's earlier batsmen gave England little reason for optimism, wicket-keeper Barnett never looking like departing until he edged one off fast bowler Farnes into the hands of Price. His score was 57, a fair enough effort for a 'night watchman'.

By then Bradman had arrived, accompanied all the way to the wicket by a standing ovation (how many Yorkshiremen, I wonder, have tried to establish for him some sort of Yorkshire antecedents?) and photographed from every angle. The Yorkshire crowd was divided. They would like to see one of the England bowlers, obviously either Bowes or Verity, get his wicket but, if any Australian was going to stay out there it might just as well be the most accepted alien who had ever played at discerning, critical Headingley. The second wish was abundantly fulfilled, the first granted somewhat belatedly. Bradman was, indeed, in a dilemma. The light was so bad that it must have been very much in his mind to appeal against it. But—if his appeal succeeded and subsequently rain fell he might regret it.

Bradman decided to conquer the conditions, which he did as only he could. He played his chanceless shots all round the ground just as if the sun shone brightly on to a perfect batsman's wicket. Indeed it looked as if Australia would build up a big lead when the light became so bad that play had to be suspended. Then Farnes and Bowes turned the game rather more in England's favour. The spectators that day truly had their money's worth. Bradman reached his century, his third in Tests that season, and then Bowes, bowling rather faster than fast-medium and with great accuracy, got his wicket, removing the middle stump—which is quite the most satisfactory way in which any bowler can dismiss a great batsman.

There was little to follow and the Australians were all out for 242, gaining a lead of only 19. Bowes had 3 wickets for 79 and Farnes 4 for 77. After some splendid bowling and even more splendid fielding by England, with the match excitingly even, our second innings was a disappointment to say the least of it. In its early stages there were ominous signs of wicket deterioration, with dust flying—evidence which did not escape Bradman, who brought on Fleetwood-Smith to join the ever dangerous O'Reilly, bowling as well as ever he did. When Hammond was caught first ball England hopes faded. Denis Compton injected some life into the innings with two 4s off O'Reilly and one off Fleetwood-Smith but when O'Reilly avenged this impertinence, having him caught behind the wicket, the England innings crumbled unceremoniously. Paynter ran out of partners and remained unbeaten with 21, leaving Australia only 105 to win. O'Reilly had taken 5 wickets for 56 runs, following his first innings analysis of 5 for 66, fully justifying the ditty adapted to suit him: 'Are you the O'Reilly who's thought of so highly? Gor Blimey, O'Reilly, you are bowling well.'

With 3 wickets down for 50, then 4 for 61, and Bradman out for 16, smiles returned all round the ground, which was packed. But it was not to be. Hassett scored 33 before Edrich caught him off Wright (whose 3 wickets, including Bradman's suggested that, had he been used earlier, the battle might have been even more enthralling). Then Barnett and Badcock calmly knocked off the few remaining runs to give the tourists victory by 5 wickets. The general verdict emerging from innumerable 'inquests' was: 'T'were a gradely game nonetheless.'

Yorkshire won the Championship, for the first time in the year of an Australian visit since 1912, such had been the calls on the county's stars tour after tour. Indeed at Headingley Yorkshire demonstrated their Championship resources by beating Middlesex without the help of Hutton and Verity, who were playing for England (to be fair Middlesex were without Compton and Edrich for the same reason). Leyland, standing in as left-arm spin bowler, took 4 wickets for 15 runs in the Middlesex first innings total of 105, which sealed their doom. Verity and Bowes were first and second in the Yorkshire bowling averages, with only one wicket and less than half a run separating them.

Hutton, though a spectator part of the season owing to his broken finger, headed the batting with 1,171 runs averaging 55·76, more than 13 runs an innings ahead of Leyland and 15 more than Sutcliffe. Smailes had the distinction of being the first Yorkshireman to achieve the double since the great days of Wilfred Rhodes and Roy Kilner.

Notwithstanding that optimistic platitude 'Peace in our time', few Britons really believed, in the summer of 1939, that war could long be averted. So that there was a deeper appreciation, at any rate among the more thoughtful, of cricket at its various levels, from the Test matches—against a lively West Indian team—to the villages, soon to be seeing some of their stalwarts in rustic Saturday afternoon action for the last time. And some fine cricket there was, with Yorkshire once more exemplars extraordinary. There seemed to be no chink in their armour, no discernible flaw. The batting was strong enough to cope with any other attack in the country on any wicket. And no side had a pair of bowlers to match Bowes, the finest new-ball manipulator extant, and Verity, the greatest practising left-hander. In fielding the team was outstanding, with more pouncing, fearless close-to-the-wicket fieldsmen than anyone could remember beholding in one side: Sellers, Yardley, Mitchell, Turner and Robinson (Ellis, not Emmott). Six batsmen, in all matches, scored more than 1,000 runs—Hutton, Sutcliffe, Leyland, Wilfred Barber, Mitchell and Yardley; Bowes, Verity and Robinson took 363 wickets between them. Yorkshire, at full strength, were unbeaten, losing only in the absence, for the Tests, of Hutton, Verity, Bowes and wicket-keeper Wood, in his last full season, which ended with his 41st birthday.

'Woody', as the genial, amusing, widely popular Arthur Wood, was, and is, affectionately addressed, played in four Test matches altogether, catching eleven of England's opponents and scoring 80 runs with a neat average of exactly 20. But his proudest claim is that he was the only man to stump Bradman. That was for Yorkshire against the Australians at Sheffield. 'Woody' recalled to me recently that Bradman had scored fifty odd when he reached forward to an off break from Smailes and overbalanced. 'I appealed' said Arthur, 'and the umpire, Alec Skelding, said "You're out, Don." Then Bradman turned to me and said: "This is the first time I have ever been stumped in my life, Woody." He knew he was out. His back foot was up in t'air. I said "Thank you, Don."' This warming incident illustrates, if any illustration is needed, the cordial relationship which always existed between Don Bradman and Yorkshire. 'Woody' kept wicket for Yorkshire in 222 consecutive matches, a record which remained to his credit until Jimmy Binks, with a total of 412, overhauled him. He also had 1,000 runs in one season and once scored a 'ton', as he recalls with relish.

Was it 'Woody' who, surveying a modern wicket-keeper standing way back to a medium-pacer, commented: 'By Gow, if I'd found myself standing back there I'd a thought I was on my holiday?' Though he liked to stand up, 'Woody' once took a catch which must have been the furthest from the stumps ever made by a wicket-keeper in first-class cricket. The match was the last Test for Hedley Verity and Kenneth Farnes. It was played at the Oval shortly before the war in which both lost their lives. Learie Constantine, for the West Indians, had scored 79 quick runs and was pushing the score along, as he could, however good the bowling. He hooked a ball from Perks which was somewhat short of a length; it soared into the sky in the direction of fine leg. 'Woody', pads, gloves and all, ran almost to the pavilion rails, where he caught it after the batsmen had run two. He was heard to observe: 'By Gow, it's lucky I were standing back.' His wit was natural, dry and redolent of the Yorkshire character. When he was asked how he had managed to bat in really bad light, he replied: 'I wasn't bothered. Mind you, I was playing 'em by Braille.'

Arthur Wood has very definite views on the 'greats' of his time. Hedley Verity, says he, was 'the best left-hand bowler I ever kept wicket to.' As Verity was 6 feet 1 inch, the ball came down from 8 feet 'straight over the top'. Expanding this theme, 'Woody' proceeded: 'Wilf Rhodes was a marvellous left-arm bowler but Patsy Hendren used to say, "I'd sooner play all day against Wilf than three overs from Verity on a sticky wicket." He was quick on his feet, two or three times quicker, was Verity.' Here are some of his further comments—On Hendren: 'Patsy were a great player.' On Sellers: 'A great skipper, useful batsman and brilliant cover-point—used to throw 'em in to me like a bullet.' On Close: 'A brilliant captain, he will take risks.' On Boycott: 'He is a good player, a dedicated batsman.' On 'ring round the wicket' field placing: 'I can see Frank Woolley or Patsy Hendren letting 'em crowd round the bat. They would have killed 'em. Wally Hammond, Herbert and Jack Hobbs would have murdered 'em.' And on the difference between Lancashire and Yorkshire: 'Yorkshire always play to win. Lancashire would say, "If we can't win, don't let us lose." We would say, "If we can't beat Lancashire, don't let them beat us." ' In his 71st year 'Woody' was elected an Honorary Life Member of Yorkshire C.C.C., a highly select band only ten strong and including Bradman, Sutcliffe, Hutton and Bowes.

Despite the absence of four players on Test duty, Yorkshire won a remarkable victory at Bramall Lane that last pre-war season. Derbyshire had the Champions all out for 83, the Pope brothers bowling unchanged. Jubilant Derby were then disposed of for just 20 runs in 40 minutes. Smurthwaite, a right-arm medium-pacer took 5 wickets for 7 runs and Smailes 4 for 11. Yorkshire then hit up 310, Barber's share being a century. Smailes, in the time remaining, took all ten Derbyshire wickets, a feat only equalled by three other Yorkshire players, Verity, Drake and Wainwright. The Bank Holiday Roses game at Headingley was played in conditions as cold and dark as the war atmosphere, now thickening hourly. Lancashire, at an infuriating snail's pace, built up a lead on the first innings, then fell, one after another, victims to Robinson, who took 8 wickets for 35 runs. The last afternoon was sheer drama. Yorkshire, needing 147, lost 2 wickets for 20, then 4 for 83 and 5 for 106. At 129 Sellers should have been easily run out. And, with Yorkshire still short of their target, a thunderstorm broke. To the eternal credit of the Lancastrians, they stayed on the field while Hutton, who had played a magnificent innings, actually scoring 100 out of 142, tried to force a win. He mis-hit Pollard in the air to the covers, racing to get two runs. Then he skied another ball, giving a difficult chance to the player with whom his name was to be linked by posterity, Cyril Washbrook. It would have been a tie if he'd held it, but he didn't. Yorkshire had won a great game and the players, soaked to the skin, raced for the shelter of the dressing rooms. Five minutes later Headingley was a lake. What a season that was for Len Hutton. In the three Tests against the West Indies, he scored 480 runs with an average of 96. He headed the county averages with a total of 2,167 runs averaging 60·19 and a highest score of 280 not out—one of twelve centuries.

The last match of the season was charged with high tension throughout. Down in the south, Yorkshire had beaten Kent and Hampshire, both by an innings, amid mounting preparations for war and the massive flight of holidaymakers from the coast. Sutcliffe, at Bournemouth, received a telegram from the War Office calling him up. The Scarborough Festival was cancelled but, nevertheless, Sellers' men proceeded to Hove. Sellers' edict was: 'We are public entertainers and we must carry on until further instructions.' It was the benefit match for Jim Parks senior, holder of the record 3,000 runs and 100 wickets in one season. The first day George Cox hit 198 in rather under three hours and Sussex totalled 387. The second day

Yorkshire replied with 392, Hutton and Yardley both scoring centuries. The third day, Sussex were dismissed for 33, Verity, bowling his last overs in first class cricket, taking 7 wickets for 9 runs and making possible a spectacular Yorkshire victory by 9 wickets.

12   The End and The Beginning

The journey back to Leeds was one which those who played in this last historic game in 1939—and still survive to recall it—can never forget. The coach left Hove as soon as possible after the end, which came early on Friday afternoon, less than 48 hours before the sombre announcement, 'We are at war.' There was none of the usual chi-iking and 'inquest' holding. In silence the team drove to—they didn't know where. It turned out to be Leicester; they decided not to go any further because of the trial black-out the Government had ordered. Clobber was left in the coach; no-one unpacked. On the way, to get on to the Great North road they had, for a short distance, driven towards London. Against them swept a fantastic stream of humanity, vehicles loaded to and above the roof with, literally for once, every-thing but the kitchen sink. Other coaches, filled with round-eyed, wondering children, cardboard gas mask cases slung round their necks, were on the way to evacuee homes. It was an orderly enough exodus but infinitely moving. Yorkshire's cricket team, one of the finest in the club's long history, dispersed as the coach reached that county on the Saturday morning, each player departing at the nearest point to home. Final handshakes were exchanged in the Leeds City square. The future was unfathomable. A great team had been irre-trievably disbanded. Sellers, Leyland and Smailes joined an artillery unit in Harrogate, Bowes and Verity the Royal Engineers, Yardley the Green Howards, Turner, Ellis Robinson and Paul Gibb, the R.A.F., Len Hutton the Army Physical Training Corps, Sutcliffe, the Royal Ordnance Corps.

Captain Hedley Verity, leading his company gallantly through a blazing cornfield in the face of machine-gun fire after the Sicily landings, was severely wounded in the chest and taken prisoner. He died of his wounds in Italy on July 31, 1943. Bill Bowes was already a prisoner of war. Yardley was wounded on the Italian mainland, Hutton met with an accident so serious that successive operations left his left arm shorter than his right—and a doubt in his mind that

he would ever play cricket again. Before the accident he had added
to his many distinctions an average of 156 at the head of the batting
in the Bradford League. Some distinguished southerners, midlanders
and others had been seen in some of those war-time League matches,
including Hobbs, Woolley, George Gunn—and Learie Constantine.

It was an aging team with many gaps which assembled for the start
of the 1946 season—and a long haul to yet another championship
under veteran Brian Sellers in his fortieth year. Leyland was now
nearly forty-six, Turner forty-four, Barber forty, and Bowes thirty-
seven. Sutcliffe, Wood and Mitchell had retired. For Sutcliffe, that
Hampshire match seven long years before, had proved to be his last
in county cricket. What an astonishing record was his—1,000 runs
in a season 24 times, twelve of them exceeding 2,000 and three 3,000;
more than 3,000 in Roses matches—more than any other batsman in
the long history of the series—149 centuries, 4,555 runs in Test
matches, 2,741 v the Australians, 50,135 career runs with an average
(over 26 years) of 52.

Like other 'halves' of great pairs, Sutcliffe contrasted sharply with
his partners. Though completely sound and technically almost faultless, he did not possess the magical artistry of Hobbs; and there was
a solemnity, an absence of any hint of flippancy about his business-
like approach and profound concentration which made Holmes, by
contrast, a jauntily jocund figure. Robertson-Glasgow, the beloved
'Crusoe', depicted them as, one like an alderman about to lay a
foundation stone, the other a perky punter off to the races. They
were, indeed, the northern counterpart of Hearne and Hendren in
the south. Sutcliffe and Hobbs, though unalike except in the neatness
of their appearance, and the incomparable efficiency with which they
could deal with menacing bowling on bad wickets, were the perfect
complement one to the other, the greatest of all opening pairs. This
was hard luck on Holmes, who was one of the most attractive as well
as prolific batsmen of his, or any other, era. He played for England
seven times in all, yet had he adorned another age, with opening
batsmen hard to find, what a different figure that might have been.
The same consideration, to be sure, applied to that most dependable,
often brilliant number two, Andrew Sandham, Surrey partner to
Hobbs, whose Test appearances were fewer than they might well
have been. The difference between Hobbs and Sutcliffe at the wicket
was once described like this—Hobbs, seeing the ball coming to him,

Above: Two more of Yorkshire's great left-arm spin bowlers: Hedley Verity (*left*) and Johnny Wardle. *Below:* Two of the most attractive characters in Yorkshire—and English—cricket. Maurice Leyland (*left*) and Arthur Wood, keeping wicket to Surrey's Laurie Fishlock.

Captains all, varying in their temperaments and approach but united in their purpose. *Above:* Norman Yardley (*left*) and Brian Sellers. *Below:* Sir Len Hutton (*left*) and Brian Close. Yardley, Hutton and Close captained England. Yardley, Close and Sellers captained Yorkshire, but Sir Leonard did not!

in that split second would say to himself, 'I should be able to hit this through the covers' (or turn it to to leg, or whatever seemed appropriate). Sutcliffe only made the shot when he *knew* he could hit it through the covers.

An odd result of the war was the chance given to a 'newcomer' to the Yorkshire team, Arthur Booth, at the age of 43. In that, his first full season of first-class cricket, he not only headed the Yorkshire, but the national bowling averages. As a slow left-arm bowler he might well have been much better known but for the supremacy of Verity in the immediate pre-war years. He took 111 wickets, at 11·61 runs each, a remarkable record for a veteran regarded, frankly, as a stopgap. The following season, his last, he took only 7 wickets costing 39·57 runs each and scored 4 runs in 6 innings. Big Bill Bowes, who had lost 4½ stones as a POW, on medical advice had to limit himself to medium pace, but he had not lost his length, his direction or his intelligent appreciation of conditions and opposing batsmen. Against Kent he took a total of 10 wickets for 49 runs, a pretty emphatic come-back. The most successful new ball bowler was 29-year-old Coxon, from Huddersfield. Hutton, apprehension about his shortened arm soon fading even if he had to make some adjustments in technique, though it was not a batsman's season, hit more than 1,300 runs for his county, including four centuries, and headed the batting with an average twenty ahead of the next player, Barber, who also topped the 1,000. The first post-war match on Yorkshire soil was, naturally, an emotional affair.

It took place at Bradford and, in spite of cold and wet, the gate receipts from a cricket-starved multitude totalled £22,793, a record. More than 5,000 members paid £4,741 in subscriptions for the privilege of supporting the county club. Yorkshire obliged the faithful by beating Kent, the margin being 192 runs. Hutton delighted the many who braved the daunting conditions, with 83 beautifully stroked runs and Leyland hit a joyous 88. Bowes, in spite of the need for caution and lack of practice, took 7 match wickets for 58 (he clearly relished meeting Kent that summer) and Robinson 8 for 49. On the same ground Yorkshire beat our Test visitors, India, by a very wide margin, Booth economically taking ten Indian wickets. But the season's 'cliff-hanger' took place at dear old Headingley which had been contemplated for the first time by returning warriors with eyes noticeably moist. Worcestershire's scores were modest, 119 and 121, Yorkshire's first innings total a little less so, 152. When a youngster of 23, John Wardle, last man in, playing in his first county match joined veteran Smailes at the wicket, Yorkshire still needed five runs to win. Excitement, understandably, was tense, the ordeal for a tyro formidable. Wardle hit a two, then Smailes hit a two. One for a tie, two for victory . . . the crowd 'froze'. Smailes hit another two and that was, breathlessly, that. At Leeds, too, Surrey were beaten by 6 wickets so that there was much satisfaction at H.Q.

13 Hutton v. South Africa

How well rewarded was a typical Headingley crowd, sombrely clad, armed with essentials such as Tadcaster ale, impervious to weather, uninhibitedly partisan, upon the occasion of the Fourth Test match, a three day affair, between England and South Africa starting on July 26, 1947. England? Hutton v South Africa was what they came to see. And they came from the wool towns and the coal towns and the dales, in dogged droves. Pudsey was silent, almost totally evacuated. It was, after all, Len Hutton's first Test match on Yorkshire soil, mature player as he was, his world record 364 at the Oval a decade behind him, his niche in cricket history secure. Woeful was the disappointment when Alan Melville, for the third time running, won the toss and South Africa batted.

But, for the Saturday multitude, which inevitably regards the Headingley Test as a purely Yorkshire affair, it was worth the wait through a patchy, often slow innings yielding no more than 175 runs and distinguished (for them) only by the catch with which Yardley dismissed Rowan for a duck. With one hour's play left, Hutton and Washbrook walked, apparently quite unconcerned, to the wicket. The crowd gave them all the encouragement of which a fervent Yorkshire crowd is capable, and that is plenty. After applauding the pair all the way to the wicket, there was a very special burst, taken up all round the ground, as Hutton took guard. He knew he had to stay there, he accepted the fact, and it never looked as if any South African bowler would shatter the inevitability of a Hutton century.

Spin and pace were treated equally with confidence bordering on nonchalance and, though the light was far from good, there were 53 runs upon the board at the close of play, no wicket had fallen, and Hutton was on his way with 32. This was sufficient to bring, on the Monday morning, zealots from the remotest outposts of the shires, and the cloth industry had to do without many a key worker.

Headingley, indeed, was well filled an hour before play was due to start when—an almighty thunderstorm flooded it. This daunting 'act

of God' proved to be no deterrent, the spectators, with true Yorkshire fortitude, streaming—literally—into the ground without
thought of shelter. And shelter was there little, a good deal less than
today, with the vast majority totally exposed, whether on wooden
benches or the grass. Soon thousands, sitting soggily on long
saturated newspapers in pools of water, were protesting at the late-
comers pressing forward to stand in front of them. 'Sit down' they
bellowed, though there was no sign of play. When the gates were
closed, 35,000 were bursting the Headingley seams and thousands
more milled around outside in melancholy frustration. Was it worth
it? Ask any survivor of that day and he, or she, will think the question plain daft. The storm held up play for an hour and a half and,
when it started with the ground visibly steaming, the humidity
enabled the bowlers, especially Tuckett, to swing the ball menacingly.
It was, without a doubt, a difficult wicket for batsmen.

However, Hutton and Washbrook, the most experienced, technically well-equipped, all-weather opening pair since Hobbs and
Sutcliffe, played every sort of ball with consummate skill. Lunch was
taken with the score 94 for no wicket, the openers having added 41
runs in an hour, good going indeed in the tricky circumstances. Soon
after lunch Hutton reached his fifty, a milestone (it could only be a
milestone on the way to a century, of course) greeted with prolonged
acclamation. At 141 the Yorkshire-Lancashire pair's highest opening
partnership up to that date, Washbrook was bowled by slow left-arm
bowler 'Tufty' Mann's faster ball and Edrich took his place. From
now on the crowd, soaked, crouching in abysmal discomfort of
which they were oblivious, cheered every run that Hutton scored.

Still he was undefeated at tea-time, the score 202 for 1, and the
crowd stayed put in its quagmire, fearful to move and lose a precious
viewpoint for the target they knew would soon be reached. They had
to wait half an hour, so tight was the bowling and aggressive the
field. Then Hutton, on 99, the vast crowd tense if not positively
overwrought, calmly, as if playing with the kids on Scarborough
sands, played a ball from the wily Athol Rowan short of deep mid-on
and was safely home. The noise of that thunderstorm was as a gentle
rumble compared with Yorkshire's tribute to the Pudsey lad who'd
done what they all knew he would do. Many spectators, not for the
first time in that unforgettable innings, had to be pushed back off the
playing area at the stern but reasonable request of the umpires.

Hutton raised cap and bat, surveying his fervent admirers with impassive if affectionate regard, and resumed, briefly, the faultless innings which had taken five hours but had ensured an English victory despite deplorable conditions. Now, facing leg-spinner Ian Smith, he played the ball to cover and started to run. Rowan fielded it and Hutton tried to get back, but slipped and fell. After that the proceedings were something of an anti-climax. Compton and Edrich, whose year of glory it was, for once failed to dazzle. Compton, like many another great player who was, to a Leeds crowd, virtually a 'foreigner' and therefore had to make the grade like a new member at a snooty golf club, had by now been 'accepted'. So the crowd was sympathetic if not wildly enthusiastic about the thirty he made. They were, however, able to relish a further purely Yorkshire achievement, Yardley scoring an attractive 36. The next day, with victory probable, he declared and the England bowlers justified his faith, dismissing South Africa for 184, only Nourse, who had scored 51 in the first innings, looked really threatening. A more modest but still truly Yorkshire crowd watched as Hutton and Washbrook steadily neared the 47 required by England for victory, very properly reached by Hutton with a majestic six to square leg.

The year 1947 was one which no-one who took any part in the game, as player, official or spectator, will ever forget. Even secretaries and committeemen, normally inclined to look on the dark side, rejoiced.

Certainly the Yorkshire administrators had cause for satisfaction even if their team had descended from the top to eighth in the county table, a temporary lapse, for sure. Their supporters had rallied in such numbers as to set up an attendance record for any county that season and a record in their own history, a massive aggregate of 278,236, a long way ahead of the 'runners-up' Kent, with 182,452. It is true that cricket provided a relief from the grey realities of the Second World War's aftermath, severe rationing of food, clothes, sweets, and shortages of everything, certainly such necessities as whisky and Yorkshire Stingo. But the summer was dry, there were no nasty bangs from V-bombs and the cricket itself was pure enchantment with Compton and Edrich hitting nearly 7,000 glorious runs between them, with Hutton proving himself the greatest opening batsman on any wickets, good or bad, since Hobbs, and Bill Bowes still, in his last season, bowling, if less fast, with much accuracy and menace.

A highlight of that splendid season, was, indeed, his benefit match

at Headingley which attracted 41,000 spectators who paid £2,817 in
gate money—an eloquent tribute to Bowes considering that the
match lasted only two days. It was, appropriately enough, a bowler's
wicket and high scores were not to be made. Bowes, as beneficiary,
tossed up with Robins, very properly won the toss and, with a
bowler's natural eagerness to get at the enemy, put Middlesex in to
bat, on a tricky wicket. He fully justified this bold decision by taking
4 wickets for 34 runs and Middlesex, thanks solely to a superb
innings of 70 by Edrich, one of the best he ever played in such
conditions, reached 124.

Yorkshire, unable to cope with their own nasty wicket, though
Norman Yardley contributed a noble 41, were all out for 85, Compton with his slow spinners and 'Chinamen' taking 4 wickets for 23,
spinner Jack Young 4 for 28. So that Middlesex had the unusual
experience of batting a second time on the first day of a match.
Edrich was again in tremendous form, hitting 102, and the Middlesex
total was a formidable, in the circumstances, 234. Bowes failed to
take a wicket this time, the most successful bowler being Wardle with
7 for 66. It certainly was a wicket to encourage spinners. Yorkshire
struggled gamely to the last, literally, for bowler Robinson at number
eleven hit 43 before being caught by Leslie Compton off brother
Denis, but were out for 186, the Londoners winning comfortably
with a whole day to spare. Nevertheless the benefit for Bowes was a
bumper £8,083, a new Yorkshire record. Everyone reckoned it to be
richly deserved, everyone, that is, except a sour spectator upon a
subsequent occasion at Hull. He was overheard to reply to a com-
panion who had commented on the fact that Bill Bowes looked well:
'Aye, you'd look well an' all, if you'd been given £8,000 for nowt.'
Strictly a minority grouse and he was lucky to escape a lynching.

Bill Bowes was, is and always will be as popular a sporting
character as you will find in all Yorkshire, big in every sense
(physically, 6 ft. 4 in. and broad to match), friendly, knowledgeable,
entertaining—whether demonstrating his considerable skill as con-
jurer and magician or just talking.

Harry Lee, no indifferent judge with his vast batting experience,
rated him the best fast bowler of his time. At his most ferocious he
was fast but he is liable to be remembered more as fast-medium, or
fast-fast-medium. From his height and with his strength the ball was
liable to rise off a length at least knuckle high which may well have
led to unworthy exaggeration of his alleged short bouncing propen-

sities in younger days. It is not unusual for a quick bowler to relish one that kicks and Bill himself has recalled to me, with that schoolboy grin which frequently illuminates a benevolent scholastic countenance, one particular kicker. In a pre-war game against Hampshire at Headingley, Jim Bailey batted long and patiently to deny Yorkshire victory. Every now and then he turned towards the old pavilion and touched his cap (Bill relates). It seemed to be directed at the skipper, the Hon. Lionel Tennyson (though it was almost certainly a mannerism for which cricketers, notably superstitious people, are famous). At any rate it rather got on Bill's nerves and he said to himself: 'My word, if I ever get the opportunity I will make one fly at you.' Twenty years passed. Bill was playing in his last match at Bournemouth—and there was Bailey at the wicket. 'I let one go,' Bill related with a chuckle. 'It missed Jim Bailey, it flashed past him and hit Brennan (the Yorkshire wicket-keeper) in the chest. He said he had never seen me bowl anything so fast. It was my last ball in first class cricket.'

There was some heavy scoring in that 'curtain' match for Bowes. Hutton hit 270 not out and Yardley 136, aggregating together 406 out of Yorkshire's 464 for 5. Hampshire made 308 and 295 for 6 and the match was drawn, but Bill Bowes had the satisfaction of a final 5 for 52 analysis, to bring his career total to 1,351 wickets economically averaging 15·68, a wonderful record. Though he was fast medium and often fast, his mentor was Wilfred Rhodes. As a boy he would watch him through field glasses, actually spotting the spin on the ball as it travelled through the air. Rhodes it was, more than anyone else, who gave him his 'deep love of cricket' to use his own words. Bill's recollections of the game for which he has such a great and abiding affection are many and lively. One concerns another devoted cricketer, A. W. Carr, Nottinghamshire and England captain. When Hedley Verity took all ten Notts wickets for ten runs, Carr was out for a duck, caught by Wilfred Barber near the boundary. He announced firmly that Verity would not do that again. But in the second innings exactly the same thing happened—Barber caught him in the deep off Verity. When he returned to the pavilion he was so cross with himself that he emptied his bag and said to the players: 'Take the lot, I've finished.' The next day, Bill recalls, Carr asked: 'Where are my things?' He was gently reminded: 'You gave them away, skipper'—and had to get a new set of clobber.

One vivid memory concerns his first game in the Yorkshire team—he was then on the Lord's staff—at the age of twenty. Through the

window of the Headingley Press Box, where we were sitting together
Bill pointed to a spot suicidally close to the wicket. 'I was put there
to field when Frank Woolley was batting,' he recalled. 'George
Macaulay was bowling and I caught him. I shot my hand out and it
stuck. I knew what a hell of a slice of luck I'd had and I felt extremely
guilty. I realised that, because I was a youngster, they had said, "He's
daft enough to go there." When the crowd applauded I felt so guilty—
it was jam.'

My own happiest recollection of Bill Bowes takes me back to a
joyous game of cricket somewhat below Test standard—on the village
green at Nun Monkton, a picturesque and remote corner of the West
Riding where the Ouse joins the Nidd. The spectators included two
farm horses named (by us) Castor and Pollux, and a sow named (by
them) Jennie, Yorkshire born and bred, to be sure, and so keen that
she insisted upon waddling out to inspect the most rugged of rustic
wickets. The game was based, as rural cricket should always be based,
upon the village inn called, after a noted racehorse, the Alice Haw-
thorne. Happily for all us southern folk W. E. Bowes was bowling,
not fast, not fast-medium, but gentle floaters. One of them, innocent
of any discernible guile, floated on to my pads as I was preparing, a
trifle tardily, to punch it through the covers. Mr Bowes, this being a
purely sporting, indeed festive occasion, refrained from appealing
for the visiting captain's wicket. I was touched. And then—exactly
the same thing happened when W. E. Bowes, of Yorkshire and
England, was at the wicket and I was bowling. Had I so much as
coughed the (our) umpire's finger would have shot heavenwards. It
was a moment of agonising decision. This, I realised, must be the
only chance ever granted to me to claim the wicket of a Test player
(it was). Swallowing hard I turned back to start my little run up.
Cheerfully oblivious of my anguish Bill Bowes carted me for six into
the pond behind Castor and Pollux—and we never got the ball back.

For sustained suspense and pendulum fortunes as well as for
batting gluttony it would be difficult to parallel the fourth Test match
against Australia at Headingley in 1948. Between the start, on the
morning of July 22 and the end, on the evening of July 27, the runs
totalled 1,723 for the loss of 31 wickets—an average of more than 55
per batsman! And England, having piled up 861 runs and led all the
way, managed to lose the game. Still, there was much rich fare for the
record-breaking crowds—158,000 during the five days, and they may
be assumed to have received their money's worth though it did tot

up to the considerable sum of £34,000. There was a mixture of pleasurable anticipation and nagging apprehension as Hutton and Washbrook walked out to what promised to be a docile wicket. Docile but—the menacing Lindwall and Miller, faster by far, than any pair of bowlers in England then, had, so far in the series, broken the first wicket partnership during their opening spell of bowling. Still, Hutton and Washbrook surely would stop that nonsense. Were they not the finest opening pair since Sutcliffe and Hobbs (Yorkshire's inevitable order of priority)? Hutton would, anyway. Hutton was warmly cheered upon his way. It was more than a normal Leeds welcome; it was a welcome back to Test cricket, too.

With a Yorkshire captain of England, Norman Yardley, and a Yorkshire number one bat, Leonard Hutton, in the middle on Yorkshire's ground, the spectators, mainly Yorkshire folk, fervently hoped for a Yorkshire triumph. The tension was evident in the silent, watchful stillness of that great throng, equipped, as always, for defence against hunger, thirst and the weather. Hutton was the first to release it a little, with a four off Miller's second over. When the 50 went up after 75 minutes and four bowling changes, the atmosphere was palpably easier. And, when, after lunch, Lindwall was hit to the boundary five times—one of these fours a cover drive of magical beauty by Hutton—there was jubilation in the air. The 100 went up, then 150. Tragedy struck at 168. Hutton was out, bowled by Lindwall just when all fears had vanished and another century on his own ground had seemed a certainty. Well, it had been a grand opening stand and the lad thoroughly deserved the ovation he received.

Washbrook went on to his century. He wasn't a Hutton, of course, there wasn't anyone in the world near him except, perhaps, that bloke Bradman, but he was a good 'un, even if he was from over the border. He was out, for 143, in the last over of the day and burly, imperturbable Alec Bedser, the chosen 'night watchman', took his place. As events proved, Bedser justified his unaccustomed status, number four for England, hitting his highest Test score and the fourth highest in England's innings, 79. He played the fast bowlers with assurance and treated the less fast without respect—fourteen runs he hit off an over from Toshack and fourteen off Johnson too, including a colossal six.

At lunch on the second day English supporters were decorously joyful, as well they might be with 360 for 2 upon the board. The run rate accelerated to two a minute by the time Edrich reached a

richly deserved century, and bowler Bedser looked like realising the
tail-ender's dream, a Test ton, when Johnson brought off an incredible
catch from his own bowling. With the score at 423 for 3 and Compton
joining his partner in all the glories of the summer before, England
looked safe, even well on the way to victory. Alas! for the best laid
plans of batsmen and bowlers, Edrich was soon out, for 111, Compton contributed 23 and Yardley 25—of the 63 runs which were all the
last seven English batsmen could contrive even on that innocent
wicket. And innocent Bedser and Pollard found it when the Australians began their innings. However, hopes soared again when Bedser
had Morris caught with his score 6, only to descend again as Neil
Harvey and Keith Miller completely mastered bowling rendered
virtually innocuous by the pitch. Harvey, if to some extent overshadowed by the sheer brilliance of Miller, nevertheless had the
immense satisfaction of a century in his first Test match. John Arlott
(in *Two Summers at the Tests*) went so far as to describe it as 'the best
innings ever played by a batsman in his first Test'. And, of Miller
he wrote: 'Miller's was not merely a great innings, but I cannot
believe it possible for a cricket brain to conceive of an innings which
could be greater.' All that, and a vigorous, confident 77 by fast
bowler Lindwall as well.

Australia were within 38 of England's total when the last wicket
fell. Hutton and Washbrook, calmly, relentlessly, carried the lead to
167—delighting a capacity crowd with a second century opening
partnership which established a new record. At the same total,
however, both lost their wickets. But, with the Lord's 'heavenly
twins', Compton and Edrich, together, the game seemed once more
to be moving in our direction. Compton, indeed, was top scorer with
66, one more than Washbrook, and Edrich had 54, three fewer than
Hutton. Bedser hit four more 4s in a lively partnership with Godfrey
Evans, whose 47 not out helped England to the reasonable total of
365. At this figure, after only three runs had been added to the
overnight score, on the morning of the last day Yardley declared the
England innings closed. His purpose was clear, to claim the right to
use the heavy roller, hoping that it would break up the bone-dry
wicket enough to take spin. Alas, again, for those best laid plans . . .
Australia's start towards the huge fourth innings target of 404 runs
with just 5¾ hours of play left, was quiet indeed. When their ration of
time had shrunk to 4¾ hours only 44 runs were on the board. A draw
looked inevitable—unless the bowlers could extract some help from

the wicket. But a draw was no good to England, already two down in the series. Win we must, and Yardley, desperate in his need for spin, tried everything, including Compton with his googlies and 'Chinamen'—and Hutton, who had only bowled 22 overs the whole season. To the horror of his devoted disciples, which meant every man, woman and child upon the Headingley ground, five full tosses in Hutton's first two overs yielded five boundaries. Ten runs came off his fourth and last over. Compton should have had Bradman's wicket and, if he had, the match might still have been ours. The Australian master edged one of his googlies and Crapp, of Gloucestershire, one of the finest of slip fielders, failed to hold the catch. After that, like a monstrous tidal wave engulfing all before it, the score moved along steadily, remorselessly, as Bradman and Arthur Morris took complete command. Crapp's lapse was not by any means the only one. Altogether eight chances were missed and the English fielding was lamentable compared with Australia's.

At tea the score was 288; by 6.15 p.m. Morris was out for 182 and Bradman was not out 173, when Harvey hit a four to bring Australia a truly great and thoroughly deserved victory by 7 wickets. The crowd, stifling disappointment, accorded triumphant Bradman a hero's ovation—after all, he was their favourite non-Yorkshire son and this was his last Test match upon their ground. Some there were whose memories went back to the two great triple centuries which are regarded in Yorkshire with almost as much pride as Hutton's own. Had Donald George Bradman been born in Pudsey instead of Cootamundra, he could scarcely command higher regard in the West Riding. Indeed he *is* one of them—an Honorary Life Member of Yorkshire C.C.C. Sir Donald himself has said since he retired that his reception on that moving occasion at Headingley was the most memorable among those he had received all over the world.

The season was memorable for that great contemporary and fellow cricketing knight, Sir Leonard Hutton, too. In championship matches alone he scored 1,565 runs, averaging 92·05, and in all games 2,654 runs with an average of almost 65. Yorkshire finished in fourth place.

14 Teenage Challenge

The last year of the tortured forties was notable, in the cricket story, for the first championship tie in sixty years, Yorkshire sharing the title with Middlesex, for Hutton's record aggregate, for the spectacular arrival of a boy of 18 from Rawdon, named Brian Close, and for the less spectacular but equally significant debut of another boy, 17-year-old Frederick S. Trueman, from Stainton. The record of achievement by the young Brian Close that year is unlikely to be beaten. He was the youngest cricketer in history to play for England, the youngest Yorkshireman to win his county cap, and the youngest performer of the cricketer's double. Another newcomer who was to make a considerable impact was F. A. Lowson. Both Close and Lowson were given a Test trial in their first season and Close got his cap for England against New Zealand at Old Trafford. He made manifest his great potential as an all-rounder in the Essex match at Headingley, which was the best possible place for a Yorkshire lad to do so. He hit 88 not out, this impressive score including a huge six off Peter Smith on to the Grandstand roof, which it penetrated to land on the balcony below. He also took 5 wickets for 58 runs in 19·5 overs, which dual feat did not go unnoticed either by the Yorkshire Committee or the England Selectors. There was much controversy at the time as to whether or not he had been 'pushed' too early. At any rate his form deteriorated in August and it was only Yorkshire's faith—abundantly justified over the next two decades—which enabled him to finish his first season in the county side and to achieve both 1,000 runs and 100 wickets.

It was a hot and glorious summer, so much so that it became fashionable all over the country for captains winning the toss to put in the opposition in the hope of a wicket or two before the greenness departed from the pitch. On a perfect summer day at Headingley, Yardley won the toss and sent Sussex in to bat. Their total, 181, seemed amply to justify a decision unlikely to be taken today, especially after Yorkshire, on the post-green pitch, had made 520 for

7, which included an undefeated 157 by J. V. Wilson, 112 by E. Lester, and 44 by B. Close hit in a quarter of an hour. When stumps were drawn Sussex had lost 3 wickets and it looked to be all over bar t'shoutin'. However, George Cox and James Langridge, the overnight batsmen, remained together at the wicket for 5½ hours. Cox, hitting 36 boundaries, reached 212 and was still not out, Langridge scored 133, Sussex topped 500 and the game was, against all the odds, left drawn.

It was a 'black ball' championship, to use a snooker term. Yorkshire had to win the last match of the season, at Newport. Middlesex had finished their programme and Yorkshire needed full points to get its determined northern nose alongside that of the Londoners. In the circumstances Yorkshire were not too happy about a total of 224, but the capture of four Glamorgan wickets for 32 runs gave weekend encouragement. Thereafter, Yorkshire resolutely forged ahead, dismissing the Welsh team in the fourth innings of the match for 69 runs, Coxon having taken the valuable wicket of Emrys Davies with the first ball of that innings, chronicled as one of the finest balls he ever bowled.

Hutton scored 1,293 runs in June to beat the previous record held by Hammond (1,281) and reached the highest aggregate of any Yorkshireman in one season, 3,429 runs, averaging 68·58 per innings. In the Leeds Test, which was drawn, he hit 101—he had the rare experience of a duck in the second innings—and, with Denis Compton (114) put on 102 for the second wicket. And an added delight for the satisfied spectators was the glorious stroke play of New Zealand's Martin Donnelly. Trueman's entry into big cricket was not noticeably fiery considering the furnace he was to become. He took 31 wickets, occupying fourth place in the county's bowling averages, and, under the heading: 'The following also batted' his figures were, 0 (not out), 0, 10, 1 (not out), 0, and 1.

Just as the thirties belonged to Yorkshire, so the fifties were Surrey's. Though runners-up five times, Yorkshire failed to win the championship between 1949 and 1959, and, in 1953, plummeted to the lowest position in the table for 64 years, thirteenth. In 1950 Lancashire and Surrey shared first place, as they had, with Notts joining them, in 1889. In 1951 Yorkshire were runners-up to Warwickshire and, thereafter for seven years, had to play second, or more humble fiddle to Surrey. Yet there was no lack of talent, no shortage of eager and able recruits to fill the gaps left by the older players retiring to coach the bright-eyed young, don the white coat, or make their way in business.

In 1950 there appeared for the first time in the Yorkshire side, Bob Appleyard, a tall, well-built 25-year-old bowler somewhere between slow-medium and medium pace, who could swing the new ball and effectively cut or spin the old. With his accuracy and ability to disguise considerable variations of pace and flight, he looked a fine prospect for a long time to come. Indeed he played in nine Tests during his short career, taking 31 wickets at an average cost a percentage point or two only above his batting average, 17. In 1951 he took more than 200 wickets but he only played in one match in the following two years. He retired in 1958 with 708 wickets costing 15·5 runs each as his creditable career record.

The West Indies were in England but there was no Headingley Test. In the Oval match Hutton was undefeated with 202 out of an England total of 344 (Compton came second to him with 44!) after the West Indies had piled up 503—surely a giant's share. And, when Yorkshire played the West Indies at Bradford, Hutton's share of two feeble totals, 91 and 127, was 27 and 91. Puny, yet the West Indians had to fight and only won by 3 wickets. Johnny Wardle took 8 wickets in the match for 94 runs, fully justifying, not for the first or the last time, Brian Close's assertion to me many years later, 'a bloody wonderful bowler with a tremendous amount of guile'. At Leeds that summer the wonder and the guile disposed of Sussex for 108 and 155, lion Wardle's share being 4 for 22 and 5 for 48, after Hutton had hit 60 of Yorkshire's 284 for 9 declared.

But, alas!, Hutton, who so thoroughly deserved a sunshine as well as a bumper benefit, had to put up with the very reverse. The match was scheduled for July 15, 17 and 18, the opponents, those chosen by so many beneficiaries, Middlesex. Rain sourly interfered with the first two days and washed out the third. Middlesex, in between the dismal showers remorselessly developing into a downpour, scored 364 for 4 wickets, the highest contributor being J. G. Dewes, with 139. Hutton had scored 5 out of 17 for Yorkshire's first wicket when the game had to be abandoned. His devoted fans collected £680 and, in spite of the miserable conditions, the benefit constituted a new and outstanding record, £9,712 6s., still the highest on Yorkshire record. Sir Leonard Hutton, 'Len' forever to Pudsey people and admirers all over the world, regarded batting as a job, not a joke. His bat, like his cap, was straighter than straight, his manner, like his ball placing, precise, his appearance, like his superb stroke play, immaculate and never flashy—often as elegant as his cover drives. His summing-up of a situation, like his defence (forward or back) was faultless. He was, and is, perhaps inclined to be reserved, yet he is by no means unfriendly or lacking in humour. As a captain he was never demonstrative but he was unquestionably in charge and proved himself a shrewd and, indeed, outstanding tactician. His hands were ever safe and he could, when necessary, bowl his leg-breaks with intelligence and guile. He was, to be sure, the compleat cricketer, with a temperament for the big occasion, the crisis, as steely as that of Wilfred Rhodes, one of his mentors.

Hutton was unflappable. The fact that he achieved the odd record of a duck in his first match for Yorkshire 2nd XI, his first for Yorkshire and his first for England failed to daunt him in the least. Sutcliffe, a shrewd judge, as Hutton himself grew to be, said of him when he had it all before him: 'He is a certainty for a place as England's opening batsman. He is a marvel, the discovery of a generation.' How right he was. More than 40,000 Hutton runs (7,000 as England's opening batsman) and 129 centuries (19 in Test matches) later he was fully entitled to assert: 'I told you so.' I never heard that he did but his protégé's success afforded him vast satisfaction.

The visits of the touring South Africans to Yorkshire in 1951 provided some agreeable memories for our now vastly experienced number one. In the Yorkshire match at Sheffield he hit 156 glorious runs in a total of 579 which gave the county a lead of more than a hundred in spite of a fine 150 by van Ryneveld. In the Headingley Test Hutton had another century off the South African bowlers, exactly 100, in England's first innings of 505. Peter May, in his first Test, scored a splendid 138 and Trevor Bailey 95. But even this tall scoring fell short of that of the South Africans. F. R. Brown had lost the toss for the eleventh time in 14 Tests and the South Africans piled up 538, their highest Test total; van Ryneveld gave another splendid, if hardly dashing, display of all-round-the-wicket batsmanship to score 236. May's maiden Test century was only the fourth in the long series between the two countries, the previous three being Compton's 163 at Nottingham in 1947, R. H. Spooner's 119 at Lord's in 1912 and L. C. Braund's 104 at Lord's in 1907.

Does luck play its part, even in a Test match? Of course it does. May's first stroke in this, his first Test, was a fluke. The ball struck the bat a glancing blow and he was off the mark. He made no such error of timing subsequently and joined the select band of Test maiden centurions. Cowdrey, in the 1956 Test, suffered the reverse luck. There was a click before he had scored and he was given out. But he felt certain there was a foot or more between bat and ball. During the lunch interval one of the Australians who had been in the slips but had not appealed, said to him: 'You know, Colin, you weren't out. I could see the space between the bat and the ball.' To which Colin replied sadly, 'I know.' And, going back further to 1930, the first ball Maurice Tate bowled to Don Bradman before he had scored, shaved the off bail. Bradman proceeded to 334.

Returning from this digression, though the Test was restricted to four days, heavy rain washing out the fifth, the attendance, 116,000, beat previous records and the receipts were a gratifying £26,000. Yorkshire, though denied the Championship so long regarded almost as their right, had pleasant enough memories of Headingley. Glamorgan were diddled out by Wardle and Appleyard for 66 and 90. Wardle's match record was 11 wickets for 58, Appleyard's 9 for 68—and Yorkshire's modest total, 210, made possible by batsman number ten, J. P. Whitehead, with 58 not out, was good enough for an innings win. Hampshire were beaten by 10 wickets, Appleyard taking 4 for 55 and 6 for 32, Yardley hitting a majestic 183 and Wardle 60.

15   Historic Occasion

The Indians, captained by V. S. Hazare, toured England in 1952 and lost all three Tests, one of them at Headingley. Apart from some notable individual performances, this was a moving and historic occasion for the very good reason that Leonard Hutton, of Pudsey, was leading his team on to his own 'mook 'eap' not only as England's captain but as England's first professional captain. Whatever Hutton felt as he took the England team out on to Headingley's green turf, having lost the toss, he did not show it. A quick tug at his sweater was the only sign of emotion, if that it can be called, he permitted himself. It was in that match that Hutton, whose every move was followed with critical assessment by those diehards who still believed that only an amateur should captain England, proved himself a leader of firmness and perception. His handling of the bowling and his field placing silenced even the most carping.

This emergence from the crucible of true-tempered steel, was a significant turning point in England's fortunes, and so, it could be said, was the burgeoning of Frederick S. Trueman as the most menacing fast bowler since Harold Larwood. This was not immediately manifest. Trueman's first two balls in Test cricket went to the boundary. His three short spells that first morning were not sensational. But Hutton well knew his potential and handled him with intelligent care. His break came that evening. When India's first innings ended at 293, after a truly heroic stand by Manjrekar (133) and Hazare (89) against a fiery and varied attack, 'deb' Trueman had taken the first 3 of his 307 Test wickets for 89 runs.

England took a modest lead over India, thanks to a graceful and competent 71 by Graveney and a lively 66 by wicket-keeper Evans. The start to India's second innings was dramatic, to say the least of it. Even those spectators most in need of nutriment left buttered teacakes uneaten as they gaped at the scoreboard. It showed that four wickets had fallen without a run being scored. A fifth went with the total 26 and then that gallant captain, Hazare, once more took a grip on the game, hitting 56 and, helped by Phadkar with 64, raised the Indian score to a respectable if inadequate 165. Trueman's part in the debacle was such as to announce to the cricketing world—here is the new fast bowler England needs. He took 4 wickets for only 27 runs. Freddie Trueman was not always to relish the Leeds wicket as he did that day. Indeed, he often found it 'bludy 'eart breakin''. The further major bowling triumphs there that year were Wardle's. He had a large share in the defeats of both Kent and Surrey, taking a total of 17 wickets in the two games. However, in the three Test matches, Trueman took 29 wickets at an average cost of 13 runs each, a spectacular enough start to a spectacular career.

Frustration was to be his lot in 1953. He was in the Services and had little first-class cricket so that, in the Test trial, on a slow pitch, he took no wickets. Statham of Lancashire, his great partner-to-be, got his place against Australia. He did not play at Headingley, however—he was twelfth man.

Hassett won the toss and put England in to bat first, a bold decision which seemed to be amply justified when Hutton, to the unspeakable horror of a dense and expectant crowd, was bowled by Lindwall with 0 on the board, and when, at the end of the day's struggle, 6 more wickets were down with the total only 142. Tom Graveney provided the only comfort in an uncomfortable and unprofitable England innings. Looking perfectly at ease he elegantly and unhurriedly gathered 55 runs out of 167. Lindwall's 35 overs brought him 5 economical wickets. The three Hs, Harvey, Hassett and Hole were the main contributors to Australia's 266, which left England with a formidable but not impossible task. Bedser had bowled splendidly, taking six wickets to beat Grimmett's then world record in all Tests, 216.

On the Saturday the gates were closed upon a crowd of 35,000 inside and a frustrated throng outside, all convinced that Len 'utton could not fail again. Those upon the inside had some brief but gratifying rewards. Hutton withstood the fury of both Lindwall and Miller, playing some beautiful strokes including a glorious square cut off Miller which Lindwall had the impudence to cut off as it streaked towards the boundary. With Edrich he saw the 50 up and then, with his score half the total, rain falling steadily, he edged a ball and wicket-keeper Langley accomplished an acrobatic catch. On the Monday the gates were closed even earlier. The fight against the bowling might of Australia, rain an ever present or hovering factor, became grimmer.

Even the normally dazzling Edrich-Compton partnership resolved itself into the sort of hard grafting Aussies appreciate even if they don't particularly enjoy it. But this was dashing stuff compared with what was to follow when the grafter of grafters Trevor (Barnacle) Bailey himself took a long lease of the wicket. For four hours and twenty-nine minutes he remained there and at the end of it all he had made just 38 runs from 17 scoring strokes off 215 balls—two 4s, one 3, one 2, and thirteen singles. It was one of his most soporifically dogged performances and expressions of gleeful relief were to be seen upon all Australian faces when Hole caught him off Davidson. Still, his tenacity gave England a chance, if not exactly a bright one.

Australia required 177 in rather under two hours, which target they failed, by 30 runs, to achieve. Their bid, however, was fraught with excitement—now they were behind the clock, now up with it. As the rate required was 90 runs per hour this was the brighter cricket so much in demand, attacking cricket with something at stake. Hutton was on the attack, too, using his spinners, Lock and Laker, as well as the tireless Bedser, in an attempt to get the wickets rather than merely to keep the runs down. At one stage 25 runs were hit in 6 minutes. With three quarters of an hour to go the Australians wanted only 66 more runs. Then it was that—after a consultation between the two of them—Hutton put Bailey on to bowl at the Kirkstall Lane end.

The legside field was packed and Bailey bowled with that defensive 'leg theory' which, when employed by a bowler so accurate and able to bowl where he likes, must deny runs.

Once more the Australians, victory so near, were foiled by the resourceful and wily Bailey—'one of the best cricket brains' as John Arlott has described him (and who will disagree?). Hutton's tactics led to some criticism, to which he replied that 'we were only playing the Australians at their own game', citing the case of Toshack in 1948, 'used almost entirely as a defensive bowler'. Anyway the great crowd enjoyed every minute (except the one occupied by their idol on his way to the pavilion run-less) of a Test match as packed with drama as any could remember. The next season, so far as Headingley was concerned, was dismal indeed, bad weather ruining the fixtures there. Gambling on its effect, Yardley put Middlesex in—and rued the day, Yorkshire failing to approach the Middlesex total in either innings.

The spinners were triumphant. Appleyard took ten wickets in the match for Yorkshire, Fred Titmus eight for Middlesex. Yorkshire

ended the summer runners-up to irresistible Surrey, as they did again
in 1955. And the match of the year, for both, took place at Headingley. Yorkshire won, by 6 wickets, what even august *Wisden* was
moved to describe as 'a thrilling struggle', in an atmosphere resem-
bling that of a Test match. This battle between the contenders for the
Championship drew 60,000 to the ground, 35,000 of them on the
Saturday. Surrey's score of 268 depended largely upon two bowlers,
Laker and Loader who, at nine and ten in the batting order, scored
55 and 81 respectively. Yorkshire's total was 166 and the odds were
heavily on the visitors when Trueman opened the bowling with
Cowan, who could be almost as fast.

Surrey capitulated to this express attack and were all out 75.
Trueman had 4 wickets for 31 (after 3 for 81 in the first innings), and
Cowan 5 for 15. Yorkshire then wiped off the needed 178 runs for the
loss of 4 wickets with just eleven minutes to spare.

The third Test match against Australia at Headingley in 1956 will
always be remembered for the triumph of Cyril Washbrook, Test
Selector and G.O.M. of the game, after much criticism of his recall
at the age of 41. He had played in his first Test, against New Zealand,
29 years earlier, and in what everyone thought to be his last, again
against New Zealand, in 1951. The storm broke on the morning after
the usual Sunday evening announcement of England's team. It was
said to be a retrograde step, a crazy way of encouraging young
talent, and an embarrassment to the captain, Peter May, who was at
a prep. school when Washbrook was opening the innings for
England. Only the Australians appeared to approve the choice.

The first morning of the match provided more fuel for the critics
and little comfort for the Selectors. Three of England's batsmen,
Peter Richardson (5), Colin Cowdrey (0—but this was cruel luck, as I
have revealed), the opening pair, and Alan Oakman, of Sussex,
playing in his first Test, were all out with the total a paltry 17. Clearly
much, if not all, depended on the verbally-battered Lancashire
captain, Washbrook, and his young and comparatively inexperi-
enced captain from Surrey, May. If Washbrook was sensitive about
the hostility to his selection (with becoming modesty he had with-
drawn from the room while his fellow-selectors discussed his late-
flowering merits) he did not show it.

With elegant confidence he scored the first boundary of the match,
an exquisite late cut off the menacing Archer, who had taken those
first three wickets. May, understandably with such a weight of

responsibility on young, if powerful shoulders, started cautiously but soon was playing with superb confidence as, indeed, was Washbrook. May reached his fifty with a four, his sixth up to then, one of which, a cover drive of pure delight, off Benaud, will not be soon forgotten by those privileged to see it. Washbrook, the 'crazy' choice, reached his fifty off the first ball of Lindwall's second spell and he had by then hit eight 4s which included down-on-the-knee sweeps reminiscent of the young Denis Compton. By 3.30 p.m. gloom around the Headingley stands had turned to something as near to jubilation as was conceivable with no Yorkshireman out there in the middle.

The May-Washbrook partnership, begun in a crisis, had reached 100 in just 132 minutes. There was even a suggestion of desperation in the changing of the bowling, the switching of ends by which means Ian Johnson sought to break the stand. The pair, despite the 17 years difference in their ages, showed no difference in agility, galloping up and down the pitch, by now showing the familiar Headingley brown, denoting docility, rather than the green of the morning, with unpredictable devils in it. Indeed, it could be said of many a Headingley wicket: 'Green pitch at morning, batsman's warning; brown pitch at night, batsman's delight.' At any rate the scoreboard showed a total of 140 when tea was taken, the batsmen precisely level with 65 runs each.

This courteous equality continued into the evening. Washbrook and May were on 70, 75 and 76 together. 'Slasher' Mackay and Archer subdued both with a succession of maidens before Washbrook on-drove the latter to put up 150, after which May took the lead. A cover drive to the boundary followed by a graceful shot to leg brought him his century, surely one of the best, and certainly most vitally needed, in his distinguished career. It also brought up the 200. But, with his score 101, May was out to a brilliant catch, low down at leg slip, off what has been described as the worst ball of the day, a full toss delivered by the Australian captain. Australian joy was unconfined, especially as this dolorous exit took place five minutes before stumps. The dependable Tony Lock shouldered the night watchman's burden and, resuming next day, looked rather more of a batsman than some of the 'regulars'.

But it was Washbrook the Aussies were after. And, to the dismay of a considerable crowd for once predisposed to an alien from across the frontier, he was l.b.w. to Benaud with his score at 98. The ovation he received could almost be heard in the Committee Room

at Lord's whence there seemed to be faintly echoed, 'We told you so.'
Old enemies, English and Australian, Yorkist and Lancastrian,
ceased all hostilities to join together in tribute to the man who came
back. Lock's valuable resistance broke down when he was 21 and
Doug Insole, in the third Test of his career, did not remain long.
With England 248 for 7, modified confidence was restored to the
Australians. But Trevor Bailey was still there so that chicken
counting was deemed inadvisable. With Godfrey Evans hitting the
ball hard and often, reaching a valuable 40, the score was pushed
past 300. And Bailey was still undefeated with 33 runs to his credit
when England's up-and-down innings ended at 325. A fair total,
to be sure, but not unattainable by an Australian side of much
batting potential and a morale boosting Lord's Test win behind
them.

But—to the delight of the Leeds spectators, it was a Yorkshireman's turn. Freddie Trueman, sensing as he must always, the fervent
warmth of his united fans, bowled with that ferocity which fully
earned him the title, 'Fiery Fred'. With the Australian score 2 he had
McDonald, the Australian number one, caught by Evans. Eight
good overs he bowled and, though he reaped no further reward, he
rejoiced Yorkshire hearts with a vital catch to dismiss Neil Harvey
when he had scored 11. In that memorable match, in fact, he held
four catches as well as getting rid of McDonald a second time, so
that his contributions, on his own native soil, were not inconsiderable. But it was a Yorkshireman the county had foolishly allowed to
join the southern folk, Jim Laker, and his terrible twin (from the
point of view of non-Surrey cricketers) Tony Lock, who wrought the
destruction of Australia. The weather had by now deteriorated. It
was a day for sweaters, with a keen wind blowing across the pitch—
which was clearly crumbling.

When bad light finally stopped play on Friday evening, Australia
still wanted 95 to save the follow-on. Then the rains came, in such
force that Saturday's play was entirely washed out. Considering that
there had been 48 hours of downpour, the wicket recovered sur-
prisingly quickly on the Monday, so that play was started at 12.45.
Miller and Benaud batted soundly, mixed defence with almost
cavalier freedom on a difficult, though by no means impossible
wicket, to put on 72 runs. But when Benaud left, caught by Oakman
off Laker for 30, and Miller, one run later, was bowled by Laker for
41, Australian hopes of saving the follow-on vanished. Lock polished

off the tail-enders, taking 4 wickets for 41 runs. Laker's figures were 5 for 58, Australia's total 143.

The second innings started little better than the first, Trueman bowling McDonald at 10. And then the first innings pattern was repeated. Harvey was much more successful and, with Miller (whose two 6s, after one in the first innings enlivened a palpably losing battle) kept the game alive until the last day, which started with Australia 93 for 2. Harvey's innings, which ended at 69, was understandably slow but must rank among his most valuable batting feats. Miller's share of Australia's 140 was 26, Burke (after 41 in the first innings) hit 16, and the other 8 batsmen had 18 runs between them. Laker had what might be described as a useful work-out for his immortal feat in the Fourth Test at Old Trafford, when his figures were 9 for 37 and 10 for 53, the clumsy if complimentary word 'Lakerised' was invented, and England won by an even greater margin, an innings and 170 runs.

At Headingley, in deep gloom, climatic as well as Australia-generated, Laker finished the second innings with 6 wickets for 55 runs in 41·3 overs—11 for 113 in the match. However, England's crushing victory, by an innings and 42 runs, will always be associated, first and foremost, with Cyril Washbrook, the man who came back, conquered, and confounded them all.

Freddie Trueman had a modest, though useful, share in the defeat by England of the West Indies, captained by J. D. Goddard, at Headingley in 1957. He took two useful wickets in each of the West Indians' dispiriting innings of 142 and 132. But the outstanding bowling achievements was that of Peter Loader, who did the hat-trick, joining only fifteen other bowlers to have done so in a Test.

England's captain, Peter May, scored 69, Colin Cowdrey and David Sheppard ('The Rev', now 'the Bish') 68 each to ensure victory by an innings and 5 runs—one of three wins, the other two Tests being drawn. On that day of the Loader hat-trick, Frank Worrell (the late Sir Frank) had batted on and on, fighting a rear-guard action. When the West Indies followed on, Worrell appeared at the wicket once more. The light was very bad but the sporting West Indians did not appeal against it. Cowdrey, in the slips, said to him: 'Hullo, Frank, I think we've had enough of you for one day!' Worrell grinned and replied cheerfully: 'I've just come out here to develop a few photographs.'

16 Trueman's Match

Under W. H. H. (Billy) Sutcliffe, Yorkshire finished third in the Championship in 1957, with Willie Watson top of the batting and Trueman top of the bowling. Unfortunately Sutcliffe was not available the following year and, to the surprise of the cricket world, an 'unknown' (outside Yorkshire) J. R. Burnet, from the Second XI was, with the full support of the Yorkshire Committee, appointed captain, which enabled him to make his debut in first class cricket at the age of 39. He was regarded as (in the words of *Wisden*) the man 'needed to restore the team spirit and determination which made Yorkshire such a powerful force between the wars'. He had, in fact, done a good job of team-building in the lower echelon, which led to a Minor Counties Championship for Yorkshire 2nd. It was not an easy year, though he did prove himself, as the Committee believed he would, a good disciplinarian.

Lancashire won handsomely at Leeds, Brian Statham taking 9 Yorkshire wickets for a paltry 45. This was a depressing experience for a new skipper. But the unhappiest aspect of the unhappy season was the abrupt termination of Johnny Wardle's engagement amid much controversy and widespread regret. He had been told that his services would not be required for 1959 and he thereupon wrote a series of newspaper articles in which he criticised the running of the county club. The Yorkshire Committee decided that this constituted a breach of contract with the club so that Wardle was no longer a Yorkshire player. He did not appear for the county after August 1 and subsequently joined Nelson in the Lancashire League.

His departure was, without a doubt, a heavy blow for Yorkshire. Certainly he was a strong personality who brought much humour to the cricket field—but who can deny that Yorkshire teams have always contained strong personalities, from Tom Emmett to Emmott Robinson, Trueman and Close. He was not only much missed on the field of play—1,537 wickets at 17·66 runs each and nearly 6,000 from the bat in 361 completed innings is no negligible contribution to any county side's success—but off it, too. Like Trueman, Wardle came from mining folk and like him again, possessed spontaneous humour more, perhaps, expressed in hilarious, cheeky little bits of mime than the off-the-cuff quip. Two examples may be cited. The first was his 'act' after Lindwall had hit him painfully on the thigh; ruefully he rubbed—his elbow. And that was at Lord's, if you please. The second was an occasion when he mimed chalking the bottom of his bat as if after a mis-cue at snooker; the ball having soared perilously over cover's head. Perhaps Johnny Wardle may have allowed his personality to reveal itself at inauspicious moments but—those who played with him have since declared to me emphatically: 'Johnny was alright and he ought to have gone on playing cricket for years.' Close puts him among the truly great spinners of his generation—an assessment supported by his Test record of 102 wickets in 28 Tests at a cost of 20 runs each (much the same as his batting average).

From the 'office' point of view no-one could have been more cooperative. Secretary Nash knew that if he asked Johnny to attend some function (which can be a bore!) he would agree and would not charge a fee or even expenses. He was doing a chore for Yorkshire, which was good enough for him.

One happy aspect of the Headingley story in 1958 was the decisive Test victory there over New Zealand. The ground had been saturated by monsoon-like rain so that play was not possible until the third day. J. R. Reid, the New Zealand captain, won the toss and elected to bat, a disastrous decision as Laker (5 for 17) and Lock (4 for 14) spun his team out for 67. England then hit 267 for 2 wickets, at which juncture Peter May, 113 not out, declared the innings closed. C. A. Milton, of Gloucestershire, also scored a century, earning himself distinction thereby; it was his first Test match. Laker and Lock thereupon repeated their onslaught, dismissing New Zealand a second time, Lock having the bigger share of the spoils, 7 wickets for 51 runs.

Yorkshire supporters, however, prefer to forget 1958 altogether. In addition to Wardle's wretched departure, Willie Watson was allowed to go to Leicestershire which county (like Ray Illingworth later) he served with distinction as captain, and the club also decided not to re-engage Appleyard and Cowan, both of whom had served the county so well with the ball. On top of all this, and at the end of a season in which Yorkshire were hit harder than most counties by the persistently atrocious weather (receipts were down by almost

£5,000 compared with the year before), fire destroyed the clock tower and Press box.

So it was with mild apprehension as well as renewed determination that the newly constituted Yorkshire side faced 1959. Ronnie Burnet was again captain and, with cheerful resolution, the backing of the players and the help of that experienced senior pro Brian Close, proved that you do not need to be a top flight performer to be a good skipper, by leading Yorkshire back to the Championship. It was very much a team effort in the old tradition. Five Yorkshire batsmen scored more than 1,000 runs, five bowlers took more than 50 wickets. Of Illingworth, *Wisden*, nominating him one of the 'Five Cricketers of the Year' wrote: 'He played a major part in almost every big victory.'

At Headingley England soundly beat India and a large crowd rejoiced in Cowdrey's majestic 160 almost (if not quite) as much as in Close's 4 wickets. At Leeds, too, Yorkshire, coming from well behind, beat Kent. Close played a massive part with 8 Kent wickets for 41 in Kent's second innings and a score of 52 in Yorkshire's second innings. But the match to remember in a great and rich year—which was also, it may be recalled, a great and rich year for many wines—was the Yorkshire/Sussex game at the season's end, the match which decided the Championship. Sellers had sent a telegram to Hove which read: 'Get stuck in, lads,' and get stuck in they did. With seven minutes of the game, and the 1959 season, left, they achieved the 'impossible', having reached their daunting target, 218 runs, in 105 minutes. In that unforgettable last innings W. B. Stott and D. E. V. Padgett got stuck in so quickly that 15 runs came in the first over. The fifty went up in 20 minutes, the hundred in 43 minutes and a hundred and fifty in 63 minutes. Stott hit 96 and Padgett 79. Trueman, promoted to have a go, helped with a lightning eleven.

Moving into the 1960s, Burnet having accomplished what he had been asked to do, handed over to J. V. (Vic) Wilson, also, by an odd coincidence, 39 years old, and the first professional captain since Tom Emmett in 1882. This burly but soft-voiced farmer had been playing for the county since 1946 and had 18,000 runs behind him. The appointment was somewhat of a surprise as his previous season had been disappointing and he had descended into the 2nd XI. But he had some splendid assets in addition to his left-hand batting and right-arm bowling, including brilliance as a close-in fielder and deep knowledge, not only of his team but of his team's opponents. Vic

Wilson caused some misgivings when, in his first match as captain, he declared with all first innings wickets standing, and then lost the match to Surrey after instructing his batsmen to go for the runs. However, his firmness and vast experience lent such authority to his subsequent captaincy that another Championship was assured.

The third Test match of the 1961 Australian tour, played at Headingley on July 6, 7 and 8, will be recalled in England primarily for Trueman's great bowling, in Australia for the dubious quality of the wicket, which Ray Lindwall scathingly described as 'not fit for any cricket above beach level'.

To take the second aspect first, Lindwall, in *The Challenging Tests*, expressed the view that the game on that wicket was 'a disgrace to Test cricket' and proceeded: 'After all, there is little satisfaction in seeing the greatest stroke players in the world prodding their way cautiously through their innings like men threading their way across a minefield with a tooth-pick.' John Arlott, in a Rothman publication, wrote: 'On a peculiar, pie-bald, chemical-ridden and shifting wicket at Leeds—for which official apologies were tendered—Trueman (11 for 88 in the match) twice bowled out Australia. 'England, he recorded, won "with slight qualms of conscience" by 8 wickets.'

Looking back on it all, *Wisden* commented: 'In the previous Tests, the Lord's ridge loaded the dice in favour of the bowlers. This time the batsmen were at the mercy of the bowlers on a white-ish green piebald surface. It had been chemically treated only a few weeks before the contest and never played true although it did not carry the same physical danger to the batsmen as the one at Lord's. The main trouble was that no-one could judge how the ball would behave. Sometimes it came through fast and low, at other times it would check in the broken soft places and stand up so that the batsmen had almost completed their strokes before establishing contact. It favoured all types of bowlers and Trueman came out triumphant.'

It was, indeed Trueman's match and, to a slightly lesser extent, Cowdrey's too. Arlott had no hesitation in describing his 93 as the finest batting performance of the match. It was, indeed, one of Cowdrey's greatest feats in that he was, throughout, facing the unpredictable. To give Trueman the credit indisputably due to him, he bowled with accuracy and hostility from the first ball (there was no loosening-up) so that wickets could very well have been his on a very different pitch. There was no reason for apprehension at the start. May, who had replaced Cowdrey as captain, lost the toss to Benaud—unlucky thirteen it was said, England having won the previous twelve—and the Australians opened sedately on what soon manifested itself as a lifeless wicket. When Lawry was l.b.w. to Lock the score was 65 and, at lunch, 77 for 1, a satisfactory if unspectacular start. And, with Australia 183 for 2 at tea time there was little rejoicing among the 20,000 spectators. Harvey, on 66, and O'Neill, 27, looked likely to be there a long time. But, within minutes of the interval the great landslide started. Leslie Jackson, Derbyshire's opening bowler, then aged 40 and replacing Statham, suffering from a strain, took the ball and was promptly square cut by Harvey to the boundary.

It still looked as if Australia were in for a big score when, off Trueman's first post-tea ball, Cowdrey held a fine catch in the gully. Minutes later Trueman had Harvey caught by Lock at backward short-leg—a real Lock 'special'. Jackson took two wickets in successive overs but it was Trueman, bowling at tremendous speed through the air, who devastated the Australians and virtually won the match in one inspired spell that fine evening. In 90 minutes eight Australian wickets fell for only 54 runs. Not only the game but the crowd, swelling minute by minute as the news spread, was transformed, from apathy to exaltation. 'Fiery Fred' was never a more apt title.

Trueman seemed to be breathing fire as, off his longest run, he pounded up to the wicket from the Kirkstall Lane end. In successive overs he had Simpson l.b.w., Benaud bowled first ball and Wally Grout caught at the wicket (a fate he had handed to many a batsman). He finished the day with 5 wickets for 58 runs and the Yorkshire crowd not only rose and roared, but surged out to meet him. It was one of the greatest receptions even Trueman ever had on his native soil.

Australia, incredibly after 187 for 2, were all out for 237. On the Friday, England's batsmen showed that the vagaries of the bowling on such a pitch could be tackled. After Geoff Pullar and Raman Subba Row had put on 54 runs in 85 minutes for the first wicket, Pullar and Cowdrey added 86 in under two hours. There were frustrations, as when May and Cowdrey found themselves unable to score for twenty minutes, but 176 for 2 at tea looked as satisfactory as had the Australian score at the same time the previous day. The score at close of play was even more so, 241, which was 4 runs on, with 6 wickets to fall. But, on the Saturday, before a 'full house'

there was another dramatic swing, England losing those 6 wickets for
only 61 runs in 85 minutes. Lock alone showed that, even on that
wicket, the ball could be thumped, hitting 30 of those 61 runs, all but
two in boundaries. England had thrown it away, the moaners
moaned. 'Wait for 'ar Fred' warned the stauncher Tykes.

The arrears were wiped off with one Australian wicket gone and the
prophets of doom, with England batting last in such conditions,
seemed to be on to something. Harvey followed his first innings 73
with a superb 53 but there was little else for the Australians to write
home about with any pleasure. When Harvey was out to a Trueman
cutter which pitched on a dusty spot the outcome was sealed.
Trueman, who had not reaped any rewards for his efforts in the
morning, had suggested to May at the lunch interval that he should
make good use of these patches by shortening his run and bowling
cutters. May had agreed. The shorter run seemed hardly to reduce
Fiery Fred's pace at all, and the result was a debacle. Once more he
bowled Benaud—for a 'pair'—and his figures for this shattering spell
were:

Overs	Maidens	Runs	Wickets
7·5	4	5	6

In fact, he took the last 5 wickets for no runs at all. Australia
were all out for 120, leaving England to score 59 runs for victory.
This they accomplished after losing Subba Row and Cowdrey.
Eighteen wickets had fallen on that unforgettable day of changing
fortunes and rarely had a Headingley Saturday crowd had such value
for money. Whatever was said about that wicket, and it was plenty,
the 75,000 enthusiasts who paid £27,723 for the privilege of watching
the proceedings had hugely enjoyed a spectacular game, with their
own hero triumphant.

By way of drama within drama, when May had been given the
captaincy instead of Cowdrey, who had led England in the previous
two Tests, there was speculation about Cowdrey's reaction—on the
part of those who didn't know him. The question was asked 'Will he
resent this treatment?' I repeat, the questioners didn't know him.
Cowdrey and May, old friends, in fact drove up to Leeds together,
taking turn and turn about at the wheel. Apart from that truly superb
93, Cowdrey assisted his successor with two magnificent catches. The
Australians had a very different story to tell after visiting Sheffield to
play Yorkshire. On a pitch easy-paced throughout, the Australians

dominated the affair and were clearly unlucky to have to settle for a draw. Bobby Simpson scored 160 and 22 out of 301 for 3 declared and 180 for 3 declared, Bill Lawry 47 and 84 not out, O'Neill 74 not out and 64. Trueman could only get one wicket for 98 runs but he scored a brisk 30 in Yorkshire's second innings, 237 for 7, in a bid to score 316 in 3½ hours.

17 Innings Unique

Trueman again took 100 wickets in 1961, and so did Illingworth. The Yorkshire batting was patchy, however, and Hampshire jauntily ousted them to win the Championship for the first time.

Altogether it was a good year for Freddie if not for some of the other Yorkshire stars. Against Derbyshire at Sheffield he took 6 wickets for 60 and 5 for 63, and scored 58 and 10. In the national averages he was placed 7th with 155 wickets—more than any other bowler except Flavell, of Worcestershire (top of the averages with 171) and Shackleton (158, fifth). His average was 19·35, compared with Illingworth's 17·90 for 128 wickets (he came third).

The following year may be said, in the Yorkshire story, to have belonged very much to Phil Sharpe, batsman and brilliant slip fielder from Shipley. He scored in all, 2,352 runs, averaging almost 41, and held 71 catches, beating the record, 70, which had stood to John Tunnicliffe's name since the beginning of the century. Sharpe, named 'Best young cricketer of the year' was hailed as a likely Test star for years to come and, indeed, had a Test average of nearly 50. He headed his county averages, which did not put him in danger of non-re-engagement, the fate of J. B. Bolus, who was allowed to leave Yorkshire for grateful Nottinghamshire. His career with Yorkshire was short. He first played in 1956 when he was 22, was capped in 1960, hit nearly 2,000 runs in 1961 and more in 1962—and was not re-engaged for 1963, when he scored (for Nottinghamshire and England) more than any other batsman, 2,190 runs with an average of 41·32. He further responded to Yorkshire's lack of enthusiasm for his services by returning from India after the tour of 1963–4 with an average of 48·87 in Test matches. A plodder, perhaps, but he could and did hook and drive with much assertion.

The Headingley Test was won very comfortably by the West Indies, Sobers confidently compiling 102 and 52, Kanhai 92 and 44. Yorkshire, without Bolus, had to be content with fifth place at the end of the 1963 season. And so to 1964 (another fine year for wine as well as cricket) when the game's unpredictability was dramatically exemplified in the early days of July at Headingley. When Dexter won the toss for the third successive time the run potential in the serene-looking wicket was such that Australia's captain, Bobby Simpson, threw up his hands in a gesture of despair. And when Boycott scored a dozen runs with gloriously confident strokes off only the fourth over of the day—from Australia's finest fast bowler, Graham McKenzie to be sure—his forebodings seemed to be ominously justified. But the innings, like the whole game, swung this way and then that. Boycott was brilliantly caught by Simpson with his score 38. Dexter hit an imperious 66, including a straight-driven four which shot past McKenzie at considerably faster pace than the express he had hopefully sent up, and was then dismissed when he had seemed at the very peak of almost contemptuous confidence, by means of a marvellous catch by wicket-keeper Grout.

Jim Parks then headed him as top scorer with 68, but the subsequent batting was pedestrian, and a total of 268 was lamentably and inexplicably short of the 600 which Denis Compton had estimated such a plumb 'un should yield us. When Australia had plodded to 129 for 1 and the Headingley crowd had resorted to glum barracking, Lawry, who had taken 5 minutes short of 3 hours over 78, was run out. A slump followed and English spirits became more buoyant. With Australia 178 for 7 surely a substantial lead was in prospect. But—Peter Burge turned the tide once more with the first Australian century of that tour. Fast bowler Hawke, at number nine, stayed with him while 103 runs were scored, then, the next day, Grout dug in to help build Australia's total to a formidable 389. Heroic Hawke and Grout each scored 37 but it was Burge's match and Burge's patient, indomitable 160—before substitute fielder Alan Rees, Leeds Rugby League player and Glamorgan cricketer, had the unforgettable experience of catching him off Trueman—which won the match. After his departure no-one had any serious doubts about the result. England laboured painfully, without inspiring a flicker of hope except when Dexter and Barrington were together and, in spite of Barrington's determined 85, were all out for 229, leaving Australia needing only 109 runs to win. With Bill Lawry out to Trueman and the score 3, that flicker glowed momentarily. But it was soon to be extinguished, Australia winning, against the odds earlier in the game, by the handsome margin of seven wickets.

Recalling that Test match has a wistful aspect. It was the last upon

Headingley victories. *Above:* The England team which beat India in the First Test in 1967. *Back row (left to right)*, Edrich, Hobbs, Snow, Higgs, D'Oliveira, Boycott. *Front row*, Murray, Barrington, Close, Graveney and Illingworth. *Below:* Gary Sobers congratulates England skipper Ray Illingworth after England had won the Third Test, and the series, v. West Indies at Headingley, 1969.

Above left: Lord Fisher, then Archbishop of Canterbury, presents a prize to Richard Hutton, Sir Len's son, in 1961—a copy of *Wisden*; *right*, John Hampshire, a fighter in the true Yorkshire mould. *Below:* The Headingley ground, packed for the England v. Australia Test in 1964.

the Headingley ground in which Freddie Trueman took part. At least he retired undefeated—with a bruised finger as a souvenir from opposing fast bowler Corling—and with his last wicket that of Bill Lawry, a considerable capture for his 'curtain'. When Freddie went out of Test cricket it was rather like dousing a fire which had been crackling and glowing, sometimes blazing, sometimes spitting, for a very long time. A fair analogy, for 'Fiery Fred' he was and ever will be all over the cricketing world. He had brought light and colour to the game for fourteen years, which would have been a good deal drabber without him. Frequently he was the centre of controversy, and 'Authority' did not always look kindly upon his outspoken comments and lack of inhibitions. But how much the presence in a team of this forthright, forceful character with such vast cricketing skill and vaster zest meant must be a matter for conjecture—but my guess is that it meant lots of lovely lolly. You couldn't mistake him from any ground's farthest confines, the broad, chunky, lithe figure, the shining black hair, the thrusting, swinging swagger in his walk, the menacing murder in his curving run-up on wide feet which seemed to shake the very earth—to deliver the ball not only with lethal power but with rhythmic, even poetic beauty of movement. Freddie Trueman may or may not be in the Max Miller tradition as a quick-fire story teller but what cannot be argued is this—he was, is and always will be a personality.

Many of the stories about him, as about all 'originals' are, no doubt, apocryphal, but more are not. On or off the field his wit was often rugged but spontaneous and highly individual. When tough Brian Close, fielding at 'suicide point', was hit smack on the forehead, the ball racing on to the boundary, Freddie commented: 'That's the first time I've never heard him shout "Catch it".' And, upon the occasion when an umpire suggested that he was cutting up the turf and courteously requested him to avoid the damage, he readily agreed. The umpire, however, was still not happy about the damage from his run, referring to it as a quagmire. Said Freddie: 'What have I got to do to bowl here, pass a driving test?' When a spectator unwisely and loudly announced that Surrey were bound to win the championship Fred addressed him with much solemnity. 'With those words you are flirting with death' he said. He even had the better, in the matter of repartee, of a speed cop who, having stopped him and inspected his driving licence enquired: 'Frederick S. Trueman—are you, by any chance, the Yorkshire and England fast bowler?' 'That's right' Freddie agreed. 'Then I'm afraid I must tell you that you are driving faster than you bowl,' said the officer. 'That I wasn't. If I had been you'd never have copped me,' was the reply.

And a classic was his comment in his last season, during the Gloucestershire match at Harrogate, when he found himself last man in. 'Can't be a bad side with a world-class bat like me going in at number eleven' he cracked. Just to show 'em, he scored 34 and, indeed, he had some useful knocks in his illustrious career, including a couple of centuries. In Test matches his total was 981 runs averaging 13·62, not to be compared with his world record 307 wickets at 21·58 apiece but not at all bad for a tail-ender. He also caught 57 Test players, exactly the same number as Sir Leonard Hutton and only one fewer than Wilfred Rhodes, Yorkshire's top Test catcher. For Yorkshire Trueman scored almost 7,000 runs averaging more than fifteen an innings, and took 1,745 wickets at an average cost of 17·13 runs.

Yorkshire fared better than England against Australia on that 1964 tour. At Sheffield the Australians declared at 295 for 8 and then put Yorkshire out for 113. But Yorkshire's second innings reached 340 for 6 before Close declared, and the Australians were struggling at 112 for 7 when stumps were drawn on the final day. The New Zealand cricketers, always popular though rarely successful—in contrast to New Zealand's often invincible Rugby footballers—must recall their visit to Yorkshire in 1965 with shudders rather than transports of joy. Yorkshire beat them by an innings at Bradford, Close hitting a century off their bowlers and claiming the wickets of 7 of their batsmen. And, in the Headingley Test match, England annihilated them, scoring 546 for 4 wickets declared and then dismissing them for 193 and 166.

John Edrich had a match to remember for ever. His share of the mammoth England total was 310, which took him 8 hours and 52 minutes and included five 6s and thirty-eight 4s—a Test record number of boundaries, beating the thirty-eight 4s hit by Sobers in his Hutton-record breaking 365 v Pakistan. This huge innings was, in the view of Colin Cowdrey, one of the most remarkable ever played. When Cowdrey went to the wicket, Edrich was on 240. Cowdrey stayed with him about an hour and was astounded to see Edrich—at that stage in his innings—play at the ball and miss three times when he must have been 'seeing it as big as a football'. He would miss altogether, then hit a sizzling four with the meat of the bat. 'It was a green wicket and the ball just wobbled about unpredictably,' Cowdrey told me afterwards.

Illingworth, in the New Zealanders' first innings, took 4 wickets for 42 runs and fast bowler Larter 4 for 66; Fred Titmus, in their second innings, had 5 for 19, including 4 in 6 balls. Yorkshire were Larter-ed at Leeds. Northamptonshire won by 58 runs through Larter's domination throughout—he took 5 wickets for 43 runs and 7 for 37. Illingworth must have impressed his future side, Leicestershire, when he took eight of their wickets, also at Leeds. Under the captaincy of that former prodigy, now near-veteran pro Brian Close, Yorkshire moved up one to fourth place on their remorseless way to the top again.

If anyone went to Headingley one fine morning in July 1966 doubting that the world's greatest all-round cricketer was Garfield St Aubrun Sobers, of Barbados, then, at the end of the game some days later, he must surely have been convinced. Gary Sobers, as the cricket world has known this zestful character for a number of years now, virtually thrashed England single-handed, with 174 glorious runs and 8 valuable and economical wickets. It is true that Seymour Nurse gave him a hand with the bat and his fast bowlers, plus the wily Lance Gibbs, with the ball, but he dominated that Test match as, in modern times, only Trueman and Bradman have dominated Tests at Yorkshire's headquarters. To go into some detail, Sobers and Nurse (137) put on 265 runs, which constituted the highest West Indies fifth wicket partnership against England. Sobers, whose third century in the series this was, hit twenty-four 4s, and scored 100 runs between lunch and tea.

He entranced the spectators with superbly confident, perfectly placed hooks, drives and square cuts. If anyone has seen more exhilarating, bullet-fast square cuts than those executed by Mr Sobers I would be interested to hear his claims—but I haven't. During that thrilling and chanceless innings Sobers passed his 1,000 runs for that summer. During the match he became the first West Indian to exceed 5,000 runs and 100 wickets in Test matches. He declared the West Indian innings closed at 500 for 9 and the subsequent massacre was not long delayed. Hall, bowling almost, if not quite, at his fastest, Griffith, and, in particular, Sobers, carried it out with ruthless efficiency. The English batting, to be sure, was frail with two exceptions, that of D'Oliveira, who scored 88 dogged runs, and tail-ender fast bowler Ken Higgs who (having taken 4 wickets for 94 runs in 43

overs, which is a lot of bowling at his speed) showed up the recognised batsmen with a bold 49 before he was caught off Sobers by his
batting partner, Nurse.

The pair had hit 137 out of England's feeble 240 and Sobers'
figures were 5 wickets for 41 runs; Hall took 3 for 47 and Griffith
2 for 37. Following on, the England team put up an even more
dismal display, to the dismay of those more loyal supporters who had
stoically stuck it out. All were out for 205, the last five wickets falling
for 77 runs. Gibbs exploited the English batting frailty, taking 6
wickets for 39 runs. Sobers' 3 wickets cost the same amount. The
Selectors took drastic action, dropping Cowdrey, Milburn, Parks,
Titmus, Underwood and Snow for the Oval Test. Snow, in fact,
played—in place of Price, who had to drop out. This time he
thoroughly justified himself with five wickets and a score of 59 not
out in England's innings-winning 527.

The Roses match at Headingley provided Yorkshire with a
resounding victory and the unrestrainedly partisan crowd with a rare
treat. Trueman and a 23-year-old fast-medium bowler named
Waring, blasted Lancashire out for 57. The latter's few appearances
for Yorkshire over the years 1963–6 brought him a total of 53
wickets. Ten of them he took in this memorable game, 3 for 23 (in
13·5 overs, of which 7 were maidens) in the first innings, and 7 for 40
in the second innings, which earned him immortality in the 'Exceptional bits of bowling' section of the Year Book. To be fair, it was
Trueman who started the red rose rot, with an opening spell of 4
wickets for 7 runs in 11 overs. His final figures in Lancashire's first
innings were 5 wickets for 18 runs in 14 overs (6 of them maidens). In
the second innings, 144, he took 2 for 26 and Yorkshire, having
declared at 196 for 9, won by ten wickets.

A rather more exciting (if disconcerting for Yorkshire people)
finish enlivened the game against Sussex at Headingley on June 18,
19 and 20. Yorkshire suffered their first defeat of the season—by 22
runs. After Sussex had scored 231 for 4 wickets—Les Lenham hit 80,
Mike Griffith, the future captain, 57 not out and Pataudi (the 'Noob')
55—the bowlers took complete charge of the proceedings. Snow's
figures were 5 for 79 and 5 for 41 in Yorkshire's 202 and 128,
Illingworth's 5 for 42 in the second Sussex innings totalling 121.

18 'Go-Slow' Rebukes

Apart from the Lancashire triumph, Yorkshire players were not anxious to be reminded of Headingley in 1966. Northamptonshire also demolished them on that ground, Lightfoot taking 7 wickets for 25 in their first innings of 175 and Sully 4 for 23 in their second effort, which yielded 123 runs. However, Yorkshire regained the Championship in spite of five defeats—the others by Surrey, Warwickshire and Northants for the second time. Boycott headed the batting averages with 39·17, and Illingworth the bowling with 85 wickets at 14·51 runs each. The following season, which started with a wet May and four out of five home fixtures rain-spoilt, Yorkshire were again Champions, though only ten points ahead of both Kent and Leicestershire. Kent, at Bradford, inflicted upon them the humiliation of dismissal for only forty, more than half the runs (22) scored by opener Ken Taylor. Kent's Graham took 6 wickets for 14 runs and Kent won easily enough on first innings. The Leicester match at Headingley was abandoned without a ball being bowled but, with the weather at last much improved, Yorkshire had the satisfaction of beating Surrey at Leeds by an innings and 92, twenty-year-old G. A. Cope, in his second season, taking 3 wickets for 30 and 5 for 23. Incidentally Surrey (or Barrington) took ample revenge at the Oval, winning by an innings and 8 runs, Barrington scoring 158 not out and taking 7 wickets.

Illingworth ended the season in quite fabulous fashion, at Harrogate, tumbling Gloucestershire out for 134 (his share 7 for 58) and 99 (Illingworth 7 for 6!) and scoring 46 going in to bat at number seven. When Gloucester batted the second time he was virtually unplayable, as his figures strongly suggest. Nine of the thirteen overs he bowled were maidens. Trueman, so near the end of his wonderful career was, sadly, without a wicket, but he held three good catches in succession off Illingworth, four altogether in the match, and he hit a brisk 34 at number eleven (as already recorded). Boycott again headed the Yorkshire batting averages (48·46) and Cope the bowling (32 wickets at 12·78 each). Boycott was also at the top of the Test averages, due largely to his 246 not out against India at Headingley—for which considerable score he had to suffer much criticism of 'loitering' and the humiliation of being dropped from England's side for the next Test.

Close, England's captain, had won the toss and decided to bat on a pitch which was good but damp at the grandstand end. Struggling for runs, England somewhat ponderously aggregated 281 for 3 on the first day, with Boycott 106 not out. He went on to compile the highest individual score in England v India Tests and his own highest score. He was then accused of 'lack of enterprise' and dropped by the Selectors, so frenzied was the current demand for 'brighter cricket'.

Boycott had opened with Edrich and certainly his batting on that first day was dour to the point of tedium, even allowing for that trickiness in the wicket during the early stages. A short, sharp shower had fallen on the wicket after the removal of the covers, making it moist. But this could hardly account for a batsman of such calibre taking an hour over his first 15 runs and another hour over the next 8. In two hours after lunch he produced a further 43. One view expressed at the time was: 'He's out of form, but what guts.' This did not prevail with the Selectors, however; nor did the fact that Boycott's second hundred, the next day, took him three hours, not six like the first. D'Oliveira hit his first century, 109, which evidently caused more satisfaction in high quarters.

The (temporary) eclipse of Boycott was not, however, the only remarkable feature of a dramatic Test match. India, 386 behind on the first innings, piled up 510 to avoid an innings defeat, Pataudi scoring 148 after 64 in the first innings (a modest total of 164), a captain's part if ever there was one. In striking contrast with England's dreary opening, the Indian batting in that second innings was sparkling and beautiful to watch. Engineer and Wadekar scored 168 in 150 minutes in a second wicket stand which established a new Indian record, Engineer reached 87 after 42 in the first innings. There had only been two previous examples of such a recovery—England's 551 v South Africa in 1947—after being 325 behind, and Pakistan's 657 for 8 (including the longest innings in Test match history, Hanif's 337 in 16 hours 39 minutes) after following on 473 behind the West Indies. Illingworth had a praiseworthy match record of 7 wickets for 131 runs in 80 overs and England won by 6 wickets with less than 3 hours to spare. Boycott reminded the Selectors that he was a batsman of some calibre with a Test average of 138, an overall average of 53·05 and an aggregate of nearly 2,000 runs. He rubbed it in at Headingley, scoring 128 against the second touring side that season, Pakistan, in a stand of 210 for Yorkshire, with Sharpe, who reached 197.

If there had been heated controversy over Boycott's go-slow batting, it was a mild discussion compared with the furore over Close's alleged go-slow tactics. Warwickshire were at home to Yorkshire. The venue was Edgbaston, which Close subsequently described as 'the graveyard of my hopes'. As the match neared its rain-interrupted end, Warwick looked like getting the runs needed. But, with five balls only to be bowled—by Hutton—they were still 16 short. Amid tremendous noise from the crowd, accusing Yorkshire of time wasting during those last few overs of the match, seven runs were scored and the game was drawn. Close denied emphatically that he had at any time deliberately told his bowlers to go slow. Nevertheless, he was summoned to Lord's to appear before the Executive Committee consisting of former county captains. Arthur Gilligan was in the chair and Brian Sellers represented Yorkshire. To the astonishment of Close himself and a good many other people the Committee condemned him in no uncertain terms: 'We came to the unanimous decision that the Yorkshire team had used delaying tactics during the second Warwickshire innings and that these tactics constituted unfair play and were against the best interests of the game. Furthermore the Committee held the captain, Brian Close, entirely responsible for these tactics. They have, therefore, severely censured him and their decision will be conveyed to the Yorkshire C.C.C.'

Close, as he wrote afterwards (in his book *Close to Cricket*) told Sellers he was ready to quit but Sellers 'with the baleful glare which pre-war cricketers tell me reduced strong men to putty in his hands replied, "This isn't the end. You have a job of work to do. Get over there and get stuck in."' That job of work was the final Test against Pakistan at the Oval. Close put the Pakistanis in and England won by 8 wickets to clinch the series—but Close was not asked to captain the M.C.C. team in the West Indies that winter.

Which brings us to 1968 and the understandable, if not altogether rational wrath of the Headingley faithful at the leaving out of Sharpe in the Test match against Australia. The unfortunate victim of this resentment was young Keith Fletcher, of Essex. The crowd, to a man, woman, boy, girl and dog appeared to be convinced that had Sharpe been in the slips instead of Fletcher, some quite outside catching chances would undoubtedly have been taken. Fletcher's failure in his first Test innings added conviction to suspicion that a cardinal blunder had been made . . .

19 'Your Committee Regrets...'

As Fletcher is both a fine slip field (though I will not assert that he is better than Sharpe) and a batsman of considerable potential, the hostile atmosphere manifest at Headingley in 1968 was less than fair. But, well, in big cricket you have to take it all, including Yorkshire's tough, uncompromising Yorkshireness. Even Denis Compton had to put up with it. Headingley was no favourite ground of his and he was no favourite there until—an apparently impossible catch at extra cover made him almost, if not quite, one of them. Barracking is not often the resort of the dedicated but often dour and critical Headingleyites. But it is certainly not unknown. On one occasion when Yorkshire were making little impression on the visiting batsmen, someone in the crowd shouted: 'Put on Hutton.' Someone else advised: 'Put on the roller,' and a third spectator capped the lot with 'Put on the clock and let's all go home.'

Poor Fletcher staged a modest batting recovery in England's second innings and was not out 23 when the daunting task of scoring 326 runs in 4 hours 55 minutes proved too great. Barrington was the other 'not out' with 46 (after 49 in England's first innings total of 302) a fair share of the 230 for 4 which was on the board when the game ended. Australia, it must be said, concentrated heavily on defence and were obviously content, from start to finish, with a draw, the sole object being to retain the 'Ashes'. I have argued elsewhere that if ever a match underlined the stultifying effect of that archaic trophy this was it. Playing for the 'Ashes' and playing entertaining cricket too often are just not compatible.

There were, however, some combined feats on behalf of England worthy of notice. Roger Prideaux and John Edrich opened soundly with 123, a first wicket stand all too rare since the days of Hutton and Washbrook and, before them, Hobbs and Sutcliffe. And local lad (then) Ray Illingworth, in Australia's second innings (dominated, as was the first, by Chappell and Redpath who aggregated 286 runs between them in the match) took 6 wickets for 87 runs. His 'partner' in this feat was Alan Knott, who stumped three Australian batsmen off his bowling—he caught a fourth off a ball from his Kent colleague, Underwood.

Trueman showed, in the Lancashire match, that there was fire in the old Fred yet, his analyses being 5 for 45 and 3 for 17. Yorkshire won by an innings, Padgett hitting 105 and Taylor 85 in their 348 total. These two treated the Middlesex bowlers with equal disdain on the same ground, hitting 136 and 51 respectively. Close declared with the Yorkshire score 358 for 7 wickets and Middlesex had the mortifying experience of being diddled out twice by Illingworth and Don Wilson. Their first innings amounted to 59, Illingworth having splendid figures, 5 for 26, Wilson 4 for 23. The second Middlesex innings reached 143, Wilson giving one of his best performances with 7 wickets for 36. Illingworth accounted for the other three at a cost of 29 runs. Boycott headed the Yorkshire averages with an impressive 77·40. Jimmy Binks, the wicket-keeper, who had beaten Arthur Wood's great record of appearances for Yorkshire and has been, in the opinion of all Yorkshiremen and many 'outsiders' unlucky not to have played regularly for England, claimed 70 victims, 53 stumped and 17 caught.

Don Wilson was the leading bowler with 102 wickets averaging 12·50 runs each, though he was headed in the list by newcomer Cope, whose twenty wickets cost 10·55 each, slightly cheaper than the forty he took for the 2nd XI in the Minor Counties Championship. A. G. Nicholson, right-arm fast-medium bowler who first played for the county in 1962 and was capped the following year, achieved the best bowling feat of the season, 8 for 22 v Kent. Two youngsters who would seem to have bright futures, perhaps in Test cricket, headed the successful 2nd XI's batting and bowling—both appeared in the 1st team too—Barry Leadbeater, opening bat, and Christopher Old, opening bowler, fast-medium to fast. They were to be seen more frequently in 1969, when Yorkshire's team obviously felt keenly the loss of Trueman and Ken Taylor, retired, and Illingworth, removed to Leicestershire. Good wishes were expressed to all of them in the annual report contained in the *Year Book*, which recorded: 'Your Committee regrets that the time has come for the great hearted Freddie Trueman to retire. He has been one of the outstanding cricketers of all time and will be greatly missed.

'Your Committee also regrets that K. Taylor has retired and is to emigrate to South Africa and that R. Illingworth has decided to

leave the County Team, especially as his decision is due to dissatis-
faction with the terms of his engagement.' During the season, too,
Boycott, Sharpe and Hampshire were out of the Yorkshire team,
playing for England so that it was scarcely surprising that Yorkshire
slumped in the Championship table and failed to gain much distinction in the Players Sunday League.

For the first time ever, Yorkshire, during this somewhat depressing
(for Yorkshiremen) season appeared at the bottom of the County
table. Bill Bowes, in the Press Box at Leeds, had to put up with some
leg-pulling: 'What's t'matter, Bill, have they got t'table upside
down?' was one crack. This position was later improved upon, but it
was not one of Yorkshire's better years. There was, of course, the
compensation of a fine win in the Gillette Cup Final at a ticket-only
gates shut, packed and excited Lord's. There was a touch of irony
about the juxtaposition, in one newspaper, of the two counties
Leicestershire and Yorkshire, displaying their end-of-season averages.
Leicester appeared immediately above Yorkshire—and Illingworth
headed both the batting and the bowling.

Not that there was any despair in the Yorkshire camp. High
hopes were pinned on the younger players, Leadbeater, Old and
Cope, nobody doubted that Boycott had many, many runs ahead of
him and every Yorkshire supporter hoped that Richard Hutton, son
of Sir Leonard, who gained his cap in 1964 and was regarded as a
possible future England all-rounder, would yet 'come good' after a
couple of discouraging seasons. Right-arm fast-medium bowler
Hutton's 7 for 15 against Worcestershire and batsman Hutton's 75
against New Zealand renewed hopes, and must have boosted his
confidence too. 'They'll get back to t'top,' is what Yorkshire's devout
followers were saying at the end of 1969's season—and remarks more
forceful if anyone expressed scepticism.

This Yorkshire toughness, resilience and constant demand for the
best and nothing but the best, does not apply only to spectators at the
Tests and major county matches; it can be evident when the cricket
League sides—or, come to that, the Rugby League teams—are
playing at Headingley. League cricket, in which the boy Brian Close
first experienced the big match atmosphere, with its demands on
concentration and self-discipline, has been the crucible for many of
Yorkshire's greatest players. Indeed it is no exaggeration to assert,
as will many a Yorkshireman, that the strength and enthusiasm of the
Leagues has been a potent factor in the success of the county. League

cricket draws its fervent and studious followers in considerable numbers to Headingley and other grounds all over the county on Saturday afternoons, and other days too—Close, as a schoolboy, played there on Tuesdays as well.

Followers of a League side such as Leeds expect from the players as high a standard, certainly in the field, as they expect from the county players. And with the publicity leading teams inevitably attract, young cricketers need the right temperament as well as proficiency kept at a high pitch through constant practice, to win approval or even to survive. The best are soon spotted and taken under the wing of a shrewd and dedicated old Yorkshire pro in the Headingley nets. And, after long enough hardening in the 'crucible', the chosen have a trial in Yorkshire 2nd, on the way, if they are really up to it, to the County team.

The outstanding players in those great Championship winning sides of the 1930s all had League experience behind them—Sellers himself, Sutcliffe, Barber, Wood and Hutton in the Bradford League, Leyland, Verity, Turner and Smailes in the Yorkshire Council. More recently Trueman (who, oddly, was not as successful in League as in County cricket) and Boycott, both came up this traditional way. Indeed Boycott was so dedicated that he would wait hours after a match ended for the chance of a quarter of an hour in the nets. Geoff Boycott, bespectacled, studious looking, reminding one a little of Bill Bowes in his younger days, can be said to have made himself into an opening bat by sheer determination and single-minded application. Almost from his toddling days in his home town, Fitzwilliam, Geoff Boycott spent some hours of every day, winter and summer, with a bat in his hand, playing a tennis ball rebounding from a wall if there was no-one to bowl to him. He was twenty-one when he first played for Yorkshire in 1962, twenty-two when he received his cap and was voted 'Best young cricketer of the year' by the Cricket Writers' Club. He received the award, as I a fellow guest, witnessed, with the modesty which always characterises him. Boycott has never been spectacular. Not for him the massive Milburn hook or the incomparable Compton sweep, though forcing the ball away from the leg stump may be regarded as a Boycott speciality. But that he is one of the soundest of opening batsmen, certainly since the war, there can be no doubt.

He is not disturbed by a 'let off'. Indeed he will profit from a dropped catch, crouching over the bat he holds rather low down, and you can sense the determination not to make such a silly mistake again. His bad patch during the West Indies tour of 1969, when he had three Test failures in a row, did not sap his self confidence, though he was naturally somewhat downcast—as have been so many great players before him, when experiencing a bad patch which seems to be going on for ever—Compton and Patsy Hendren among them.

20 After Seventy Years

Just seventy years after the first ever Test match at Headingley, the West Indians were welcomed to the now venerable ground. Changes there had been in three score years and ten, changes such as the new pavilion cum office building—this change not universally welcomed. One famous cricketer, indeed, who mourns the old one is England's cricket captain, Colin Cowdrey. As he strode out of that old building he was, in his mind, following in the footsteps of the illustrious, of Don Bradman, Herbert Sutcliffe, Jack Hobbs, Frank Woolley and earlier heroes. It was awesome, even humbling. 'It just isn't the same thing coming out of the new place,' he once said to me. 'I certainly miss the old one.' Another change saddens Cowdrey—and other batsmen, rather than bowlers, I suspect—the slowing up of the outfield. Not so many years ago the ball raced to the boundary, especially at the Grandstand end where the fieldsman, running down the slope, found it getting away from him. 'Now the grass is so green it's a job to get a four' says he.

Changes in the landscape, too, the tall, modern buildings of advancing commerce discernible behind the red brick homes and shops now clustering all round the screening walls. Changes, too, in the appearance of the devoted Headingley crowds, dressier in their well-cut suits of Huddersfield worsted, and not a clog to be seen. Mini-skirts? What would Lord Hawke have said in 1899? Not a lot of change in the dress of the players. White flannels just a trifle narrower, perhaps, but boots, shirts, caps, blazers unchanged in a changing world. Are we friendlier with our opponents than we used to be? It seemed odd, somehow, though warming to behold Gary Sobers bowling to an out-of-touch Geoff Boycott in the Headingley nets to help get his eye in before bowling to him in dead earnest out in the middle. Did Noble bowl to Brown to get him used to it? It seems hardly likely, if only because the professionals in those days 'knew their station' and did not mingle with the gentlemen except when actually engaged in the game on the field.

Astonishingly, there was one link that day with the Test of seventy years before and with the ground before that. Wilfred Rhodes, who first played for Yorkshire there in 1898 had made the journey north from Bournemouth to hear the match. Not only to hear it but to interpret it almost ball by ball. 'That was a good 'un, cover drive wasn't it?' he would say. And, as likely as not, he would be right.

The details of that contest between an England team which cannot be reckoned among the greatest, and a West Indian side gentle and brittle compared with the era of their ferocious invincibility do not make attractive reading for the people of Yorkshire. A considerable rather than huge crowd was reduced to dumb misery by the contemplation of a 'procession' involving four batsmen, all Yorkshiremen—Boycott, Sharpe, Hampshire and emigrant Illingworth—unable to amass between them more than sixty runs in eight innings.

A tame game utterly devoid of breathless hush became largely a battle between tail-enders, and England's tail-enders proved to be slightly better batsmen than those of the West Indies. Knott was conspicuous in this contest, scoring 44 and 31. To be fair to the 'recognised' batsmen, D'Oliveira scored 48 and 39 and Edrich gave England a reasonable start with 79 after Boycott, starting breezily enough, had been out l.b.w. to Sobers for 12. On the last day, the West Indies needed 63 runs with three wickets standing, to win the match and level the series. They fought long and dourly, number eight, Findlay, the wicket-keeper, taking 102 minutes to score 19, Holder, at number nine (joint top scorer in the first innings with 35) 47 minutes to reach 13. They failed, by 31 runs, to reach their target.

Ray Illingworth, captain of England as well as Leicestershire, very properly and understandably was warmly applauded to the wicket upon which he had accomplished so much for his native county with bat and ball. The Headingley throng, surveying him back on that familiar old 'mook 'eap' was not unaware of the irony of the situation. Here was one of Yorkshire's greatest all-rounders, never offered the leadership of his own team, not only leading that Midland lot, but England too. Like Hutton? Aye, but Hutton, though he never was captain of Yorkshire, was still a Yorkshire star when he captained England. Yorkshire folk, watching the cricket that day, were not in the mood to argue the whys and wherefores of this second Test skipper from Pudsey being allowed to leave them.

In the pubs at night, aye, great argument was to be heard. 'Stiff necked lot, the Committee. Rules is rules, they say and never mind t'player,' sums up a fairly frequently expressed view. Well, there are those who feel that some compromise could have been reached, to give Illingworth the security he felt he needed for his growing family, some relaxation of the policy which is built upon the faith and hope of the player rather than charity towards him. For Yorkshire, with that lofty confidence in itself which is so firmly embedded a characteristic of that thrusting county, says, in effect: 'If you don't want to play for us, you had better go elsewhere.' Not to want to play for Yorkshire, on whatever terms, is unimaginable. In fact it can hardly be satisfactory to know that you are re-engaged for the next season only if you have not heard to the contrary by about the middle of July. Yet that is the Yorkshire way. Those who believe in it—and it is not a question of brass, they do believe that this way ensures the true loyalty and utter dedication that wins championships—point out that the player who is told that his engagement will not be renewed is paid until the end of that year, and the player who is not so informed knows that he will be paid until the end of the following year. From Illingworth's point of view the sadness of parting was sweetened by a contract more to his liking, and honours he had not really expected.

If he had not been appointed captain of Leicestershire could he possibly have been appointed captain of England over the head of his own captain, the discarded (by Lord's) Brian Close? Indeed, the faith which the Yorkshire authorities have shown in Close, whatever the rights and wrongs of the Edgbaston incident, reflects the sturdy, abiding relationship between Committee and players in spite of any re-engagement differences. Yorkshire's attitude is, roughly: 'We look after our chaps, if they are loyal to us.' Close appreciates this trust. And he will not 'bind' about his treatment at Lord's. 'I've had my ups and downs' is about as far as he likes to go now. It was his one reference to the Lord's ordeal and the subsequent loss of England's captaincy, when we sat together during the glorious summer of 1969, in the captain's room at the top of the pavilion at Hove, looking out at a fair, rather than even middling crowd, which is as much as we can expect in mid-week nowadays.

What has provided the greatest possible satisfaction to the one-time prodigy who has confounded all normal prodigy prognostications by remaining as good a player and as modest a man year after year, is—to be captain of Yorkshire. 'I have been knocked down so many times and climbed up again. When I got the captaincy of

Yorkshire it was something extra after losing previous ambitions,' he said to me without rancour but with a pride I could sense.

As captain, Close has found that a completely different attitude to the game is necessary. As a member of a team—and he always played for the team—he had to think of what he was going to do. 'As captain you have to think for everyone else before you think for yourself' he explained. Which makes Close a very good captain. In terms of championship points Yorkshire had a lean season that year (they even lost to Sussex in that Hove game) but the Gillette Cup, like captaincy of the county, gave him 'something extra'. What he does regret, looking back to the days when, aged eleven, he was the youngest of all League players, is the discouragement of spinners implicit in 'instant cricket' and modern League cricket. All seamers, up-and-down . . . never seen spinners in League games because they are too expensive . . . all skill, thought and planning have gone out of the game . . . thus he will lament.

Well, will big matches in future be dominated by slow spinners as they were by Rhodes, Verity and Wardle? At Headingley, perhaps, if three-day county matches and five-day Test matches continue, if the wicket remains as it is, often unhelpful to the fast bowlers after the disappearance of the morning greenness and heaviness in the atmosphere allowing much movement in the air. A wicket on which bowlers 'have to work like mad', though, after rain, it will take spin. A wicket, indeed, which—apart from that period when it deteriorated so badly that Leeds nearly lost its Test matches—has produced batting records and bowling records, triple centuries and 'all tens' as well.

'I like Headingley' said the successor to Lord Hawke, Brian Sellers and Norman Yardley thoughtfully, 'I think it is a most pleasant ground.' That typically Yorkshire understatement, surely, justifies in abundance the faith and foresight of those enterprising gentlemen of Leeds who clubbed together to buy 'Lot 17a'.

Appendix One

OFFICIALS OF
THE YORKSHIRE COUNTY CRICKET CLUB

PRESIDENTS

1863	T. R. Barker
1864–1897	M. J. Ellison
1898–1938	Lord Hawke
1939–1947	Sir Stanley Jackson
1948–1960	T. L. Taylor
1961–	Sir William Worsley

TREASURERS

1863–1893	M. J. Ellison
1894–1898	M. Ellison Jun.
1899–1912	Charles Stokes
1913–1931	R. T. Heselton
1932–1962	A. Wyndham Heselton
1963–	M. G. Crawford

SECRETARIES

1863	George Padley
1864–1902	J. B. Wostinholme
1903–1928	F. C. Toone
1929–30	Sir Frederick Toone
1931–	J. H. Nash

Appendix Two

HONORARY LIFE MEMBERS OF
THE YORKSHIRE COUNTY CRICKET CLUB

Sir Donald Bradman
R. Broomhead
Wilfred Rhodes
Herbert Sutcliffe
Mrs F. Frazer
Sir Stuart Goodwin
Sir Leonard Hutton
Percy Holmes
W. E. Bowes
Arthur Wood

Patroness
H.R.H. The Duchess of Kent

Appendix Three

YORKSHIRE CAPTAINS

1863–1870	R. Iddison
1871–1875	J. Rowbotham
1876–7	E. Lockwood
1878–82	T. Emmett
1883–7	Hon. M. B. Hawke
1888–1910	Lord Hawke
1911	E. J. Radcliffe
1912–14	Sir Archibald White
1919–21	D. C. F. Burton
1922–4	G. Wilson
1925–7	Major A. W. Lupton
1928–9	Captain W. A. Worsley
1930	A. T. Barber
1931–2	F. E. Greenwood
1933–47	A. B. Sellers
1948–55	N. W. D. Yardley
1956–7	W. H. H. Sutcliffe
1958–9	J. R. Burnet
1960–2	J. V. Wilson
1963–	D. B. Close

Index